Ordnance Survey map of Sevenoaks, 1870

SEVENOAKS
PAST

with the Villages of Holmesdale

The view from the top of St Nicholas' Church at the end of the 19th century is virtually identical to today's (though there are more trees today). Six Bells Lane runs across the bottom half of the picture to its summit by the old bakery courtyard where a huge catslide roof bristling with dormers can be seen.

SEVENOAKS PAST

PAST

with the Villages of Holmesdale

Christopher Rayner

Phillimore

1997

Published by
PHILLIMORE & CO. LTD.
Shopwyke Manor Barn, Chichester, West Sussex

ISBN 1 86077 056 8

Printed and bound in Great Britain by
BIDDLES LTD.
Guildford and King's Lynn

To Lesley

Contents

List of Illustrations ix
Acknowledgements xi
Illustration Acknowledgements xii

I   Early Settlement in the Valley 1
II   The Renaming of the Landscape 11
III   The Market Economy 27
IV   New People and New Ideas 45
V   Georgian Order 59
VI   Victorian Growth 75
VII   Postscript 117

Bibliography 125
Index 127

List of Illustrations

Frontispiece: St Nicholas Church roof, aerial view

1. Halstead flint buildings 2
2. Polhill chalk pit 4
3. Chipstead's brickworks 5
4. Seal Hollow Road 6
5. Oldbury map .8
6. Lullingstone Roman villa, mosaic floor 9
7. Brasted Church .12
8. Otford pond 12
9. Polhill burial 13
10. Chevening 14
11. Shoreham bridge 15
12. Seal High Street 15
13. Knockholt Church 16
14. Penshurst 17
15. Shenden valley .18
16. Riverhead Church 19
17. Eynsford ford 20
18. Filston Hall 20
19. West Stow hut reconstruction 21
20. St Nicholas' Church and High Street 22
21. Kemsing spring .23
22. The seven oaks .25
23. Chipstead Square 25
24. Otford green 27
25. Otford Mill 29
26. Shoreham Mill .29
27. *Lamb Inn*, Sundridge 30
28. Otford court hall 31
29. Becket's well 32
30. Sevenoaks upper High Street 33
31. *Chequers Inn* 34
32. The Shambles, 1925 35
33. The Shambles, 1930 35
34. 101 High Street .36
35. 99 and 101 High Street reconstruction . . .37
36. Brasted green 38
37. Westerham green 39
38. *Bligh's Hotel* 40
39. Vine Cottage 41
40. Chiddingstone 42

41. Flemish House, Riverhead 43
42. *Amherst Arms*, Riverhead 43
43. Old Hall, Sundridge 44
44. Knole House, *c.*1860 45
45. Otford Palace 46
46. Grand staircase, Knole 49
47. Retainers' Gallery, Knole 49
48. The chapel, Knole 49
49. Bradbourne's chapel 50
50. St Clere 51
51. Park Place 52
52. Godden Green .53
53. Kemsing Old Vicarage 54
54. Westerham Buttery 55
55. Riverhead 57
56. Chipstead Place .59
57. Chipstead Place, stables 60
58. Riverhill House .60
59. Chevening House 61
60. Combe Bank, stables 61
61. Montreal House .62
62. Greatness House 62
63. Greatness millworkers' cottages 62
64. Kippington House 63
65. Brasted Place, north elevation 64
66. Brasted Place, south elevation 64
67. Bradbourne Hall 64
68. The Red House .65
69. Sevenoaks School 66
70. Longford Bridge 67
71. Chipstead Square 68
72. Watson's map, 1755 69
73. Map of the Hundred of Codsheath, 1778 .70
74. Knole ice house .71
75. Knole Lodges 71
76. Chipstead Place, West Lodge 71
77. Chipstead Place, Percy Lodge 72
78. Greatness House lodge 72
79. Wildernesse, Park Lane lodge 73
80. Kippington Lodge 74

81. *Royal Oak Hotel* 76
82. The Old Post Office 77
83. Rayley's Corner 77
84. Rayley's Corner and Six Bells Lane 78
85. The White House 78
86. Sevenoaks Coffee Tavern 79
87. West End Dairy 79
88. *Royal Crown Hotel, c.1860* 80
89. *Royal Crown Hotel, 1920s* 80
90. London Road 80
91. Lime Tree Walk coal merchant 81
92. *Dorset Arms* 81
93. Vallin's Stores 82
94. Walnut Tree House 82
95. Knott's Mill 83
96. North end of the High Street 83
97. Bethlehem Farm 84
98. *Bligh's Hotel* 84
99. 119-123 High Street 84
100. Suffolk Place brewery 85
101. Suffolk Terrace 85
102. *Holmesdale Tavern* 86
103. 113-117 High Street 86
104. Lower High Street 87
105. Martin and Dolton's shop 87
106. Market House 88
107. Bank Street 88
108. World Stores 88
109. *Rose and Crown Hotel* 89
110. High Street 90
111. The market place 91
112. Redman's Place 91
113. Warren's shop 92
114. Fire at Mr. Dray's 92
115. Vine bandstand 93
116. The Vine 93

117. Dartford Road parade 94
118. Barn fire, Knole 95
119. Lord and Lady Sackville's homecoming . . . 95
120. Knole laundry 96
121. Ashgrove 97
122. Beechmont 97
123. Wildernesse 98
124. Knockholt House 99
125. Bulimba 100
126. Carrick Grange 100
127. Construction of Vine Lodge 101
128. Tub's Hill station 102
129. Accident at Tub's Hill station 102
130. Brasted station 103
131. Emily Jackson's hip hospital 104
132. Lime Tree Walk 105
133. *Sevenoaks Chronicle* offices 106
134. Post Office, South Park 107
135. Police station 107
136. Cottage Hospital 108
137. Seal Fire Brigade 109
138. Seal Church, interior 110
139. St Nicholas' Church 110
140. Riverhead Church 111
141. Congregational Church, St John's Hill . . . 111
142. Congregational Church Hall 112
143. Vine Court 113
144. Granville Road 113
145. Dunton Green brickworks 114
146. Burrell's forge, Underriver 115
147. Dunton Green Lido 117
148. Iron Church 119
149. Golding's brewery 120
150. Otford High Street 120
151. H.G. Wells' cycle shop 121
152. Dunton Green bus station 122

Acknowledgements

I would like to give my thanks to all those who have helped me in the various stages that have led to this book.

In particular my love and thanks to Lesley, and to Tom, Joey and Mikey. Their help has been incalculable.

My late father, Michael, was born in Granville Road and grew up in Sevenoaks, later practising as an architect with an office in the town. I recall many hours spent over the years discussing old buildings with him and his memories of the town before the war.

My grateful thanks, too, to other members of the Sevenoaks Society, including Ian Abbott, who helped me with my first lectures on local architecture, and John Watts, who has helped greatly with the Society's archive photographs of the town. These have been a tremendous resource, generously donated by Gordon Anckorn, Sir John Dunlop and others, which is today still growing. Thanks also to Eric Keys, Bruce Walker, Alan Ford and Peter Rogers.

Thanks also to Amber Baylis of the Local Studies Collection at Sevenoaks library and her colleagues.

Some have helped directly or indirectly with the wider study of the qualities of places and building. My deepest thanks to Chris Royer, Chris Alexander, Stewart Brand and others.

My thanks also to Anthony Stoyel, Alan Everitt, Mike Higgins and Marian Mills, for their help in discussing problem areas with me over the past few years.

Many have helped with particular buildings or questions I have had, including William Alexander (Shoreham Castle), Vic Bowden (Kemsing), Mrs. Charlesworth (Kippington), Jonathan Fenner (local villages), Kenneth Gravett (local buildings), Sue Haydock, Diocese of Rochester (local churches), Captain David Husband (Chevening House), Graham Keevil, Oxford Archaeological Unit (St Nicholas' Church), Andrew King (Richard Rayner), Derek Lucas (Seal Church), Brigadier Maynard (Ashgrove/West Heath School), Mick Molloy (Montreal), Ronnie Norman (St Clere), Jeremy Pearce (the *Black Boy*), Gordon Raybould (Sundridge), Steve Rayner (medieval archery practice ranges), Mrs. Eve Rogers (Riverhill House), Hugh Sackville-West (Knole), Bill Soutar (Tub's Hill), Walter Stevens (Seal Church), Alan Swann (inns and public houses), Cliff Ward, Otford and District Archaeological Group (Romshead Manor), Michael Wilson (Brasted Place).

Thanks also to present and former clients who have let me work on and get to know so many historic and more recent houses, churches, and other buildings locally.

On the technical side, my thanks to Lesley again, and to my sister Caroline, Ian Storey, Mike Brill and Arthur Cooksey for advice and help. Thanks, too, to Noel Osborne and Nicola Willmot of Phillimore.

Illustration Acknowledgements

Ian Abbott, 6, 85; Myron Goldman, 47; Andrew King, 75, 140; Derek Lucas, 138; James Melcher, 54, 72; Christopher Rayner, 18, 19, 50, 73, 121; Anthony Stoyel, 35; The Sevenoaks Society, frontispiece, 3, 5, 9, 10-12, 14, 15, 17, 20-4, 26, 30-2, 34, 37-9, 44-6, 48, 53, 55, 57-60, 62, 63, 65, 66, 68, 70, 74, 76, 78-83, 89, 91-3, 96, 99, 101, 102, 104-9, 111-15, 117, 119, 120, 122-7, 131, 134, 136, 141, 142, 148, 151, endpapers; The Sevenoaks Society/G. Anckorn collection, 1, 2, 7, 8, 13, 16, 25, 27-9, 36, 41-3, 52, 56, 69, 71, 77, 116, 100, 97, 98, 118, 129, 130, 132, 133, 135, 137, 141, 142, 144-7, 149, 150, 152; The Sevenoaks Society/J. Dunlop collection, 33, 61, 64, 69, 84, 94, 95, 103, 110, 128, 139, 143.

Early Settlement in the Valley

Prehistoric and Roman Holmesdale

The story of Sevenoaks begins as the story of a river valley, the valley of the river Darent, locally called Holmesdale. The river rises in several springs around the village of Westerham and flows firstly to the east, then cuts northwards through the chalk hills to the Thames estuary.

At the end of the Ice Age, 10,000 years or so ago, this river would have been far larger than the one we see today; many streams rushed down the hills on each side to meet it. They are effectively dry today and are now followed by roads and tracks: Seal Hollow Road and Brittains Lane in Sevenoaks are river bed roads, grown up from much earlier tracks; the main railway line to Tonbridge follows another, deepened into a cutting. Sevenoaks itself is on a narrow ridge made prominent by the river valleys on either side.

The Holmesdale valley was formed when the softer gault clay was eroded between the relatively harder chalk above and the Lower Greensand strata below. The chalk now forms the North Downs scarp face, while the lower greensand outcrops on the gentler rising Chartland to the south.

The usefulness of the land to its new settlers, whether for crops, pasture or for woodland, is directly linked to the strata beneath, as is where these people would choose to live, and the materials with which they would build their homes and other structures.

The chalk Downland reaches its highest point in Kent at Westerham Hill (251m.). Ice-Age rivers have cut deep dry north-running valleys or combes into it, as at Knatts Valley, north of Kemsing. At Chevening, one valley has been carved into the face of the escarpment, creating a sheltered bowl

and an easier climb to the summit, factors that influenced one of the valley's earliest settlements below.

The chalk is mostly overlain with clay and flints, making it infertile and marginal. Its coldness and relative inaccessibility have kept it a poor area in the past, exploited for its woodland and pasture by prosperous valley communities. For much of its history, Downland settlement was limited to isolated churches and farms. Occasional ruined churches, as at Woodlands and Maplescombe to the north of Kemsing, testify to a more precarious existence. The flint has been used in various forms as the predominant building material.

Near the base of the North Downs, the chalk and a thin layer of Upper Greensand sit on the gault clay of the Holmesdale valley floor. Ground water seeping through the chalk meets the impervious layer of clay and creates a spring line here. A string of villages follows this contour line at regular intervals, including Chevening, Otford and Kemsing locally.

The valley floor gault clay is improved by downwash and mixing with the chalk and greensand on either side, and provides a fertile oasis for the earliest settlements. Another string of villages follows the river Darenth along the valley floor, although avoiding the gault clay itself. In more recent times, the clay would be useful for brick and tile production supplying local and, later, national needs.

To the south, the Chartland climbs gently up the Greensand ridge, before tumbling down into the Weald. As with the Downland, the area is cut by north-running post-glacial river valleys making travel to the east and west difficult and keeping much of it isolated. The ridge reaches its

1 Halstead village in the early years of the century shows its Downland location in the great use of local flint. The curved building corner, also seen in Shoreham, is a clever local adaptation to avoid the brickwork which would have been needed to build a 90-degree corner. In the foreground the Knockholt coach poses on its way to a local wedding.

highest point in Kent at Toys Hill (247m.), to the south of Brasted, and the general height of the rising land would make it very difficult to supply with fresh water as well depths were beyond early technologies. The stony soil causes great problems for gardeners in Sevenoaks, but once proved useful for roadstone which was dug out from the surface leaving small pits, still to be found at Oldbury Hill and other local woods. Deeper down there are ragstone seams, though not as good as in the Maidstone area, famous for its Kentish Ragstone since Roman times.

Locally quarried Kentish Rag can be found in a great number of buildings in and around Sevenoaks. A wooded pit to the west of Sundridge church may have been used to provide stone for the church or for Sundridge Place beside it. At Hosey Common near Westerham a sequence of tunnels follows good seams of hard stone up to a mile long. Bats in great numbers now live here in a sanctuary operated by the Kent Trust for Nature Conservation and occasionally open to the public. Stonepitts, an old farm near Seal, takes its name from an early stone quarrying site. The

local origin of building materials is demonstrated by the increasing rustiness, caused by the increasing iron content, of the stone that can be seen in buildings while travelling east from Sevenoaks towards Wrotham Heath.

Agriculturally, however, the Chartland was poor, and was often used as commonland, reflected in the names Hosey Common, Goathurst Common, Sevenoaks Common, and Fawke Common, typically nearer the crest of the ridge, as the common land has receded upslope over many centuries.

The scarp slope of the Greensand ridge is less steep than that of the North Downs, in places encouraging farms to be built upon it, as at Panthurst, near Sevenoaks Weald, Riverhill House, Romshed and St Julians. But it is an unreliable slope, subject to creeping and slumping caused by the lubrication of the springline over the clay at its base. This has affected some garden walls at Riverhill House, and caused very serious problems for the Sevenoaks Bypass bridge builders at Hubbards Hill. This was as nothing compared with the landslip at Crockham Hill in

1596, when 22 hectares of land moved 20m. over 11 days, or even a later smaller slip at Toys Hill in 1756. The trees that still cover much of the scarp are possibly relics of original woodland that covered the Weald and Chartlands, and contain one of the ancient woodland indicator species, yellow archangel.

For countless thousands of years it is likely that only hunters knew the site of Sevenoaks. The caves on the east side of Oldbury Hill, between Seal and Ightham, were occupied during the Ice Age by early Stone-Age hunters whose limited tools made caves very attractive dwellings, although their true size may be misunderstood today as over time they filled up with sediment and lost projecting roof sections. Another group of caves occupied in this way was at Stonewall in Chiddingstone.

These earliest Palaeolithic peoples may have visited the area to hunt in the summer, returning across the land bridge to mainland Europe for the winter. More sustained occupation of the land has happened in the last 10,000 years with the rise in summer temperature to around 15°C, allowing hunting of elk, wild cattle and horse in summer months and reindeer in winter.

Mesolithic flint factories, where remaining fragments or microliths show extensive shaping of flint tools, have been found in the vicinity of Chipstead Place and in Packhorse Road nearby. These may have been near settlement sites, and certainly at Blackhall, on the north-east edge of Sevenoaks, evidence exists of later Neolithic and Bronze-Age occupation, though we cannot tell whether this was continuous. Other Mesolithic material has been found on the tumulus at Millpond Wood at Greatness and at Greenhill above Otford, high sites from where the movements of deer and large game could be watched. Odd flint blades have also been found recently in Westerham Road in Chevening, Lyndhurst Drive and St John's Hill in Sevenoaks, and elsewhere, perhaps left where they fell during a hunt.

These early settlements were probably small, close family groups relying on hunting and gathering, and later on animal husbandry and limited cultivation. Their homes would have been simple shelters of poles, with perhaps the gaps filled with earth and dung, and with a light roof of straw or turf, or they may have been covered

with animal skins. Such buildings do not last long, which may have been intentional, as the hunters followed the seasonal migrations of their animals or slash-burned new areas of forest for short-term cultivation.

The 'Neolithic revolution', from 3000 B.C. onwards, was brought about by advances in agriculture through the use of tools and the domestication of animals, and in material crafts such as pottery, spinning and weaving. Axes and arrowheads have been found at Blackhall, at the former Otford Road refuse tip, and along the Downs above Kemsing and Otford, suggesting early farms in all of these places.

These people would have lived primarily on the well-drained gravel sites near the River Darent. Its name is one of the handful of Celtic or pre-Roman names to have survived Saxon renaming in the South East, and means 'oak stream'. It would have been much faster running in Neolithic times as the sea level was lower. Other settlements were near the spring line near the foot of the Downs where a prehistoric trackway followed a route much the same as the present Pilgrims' Way, with another ancient trackway above on the hill crest. There would also have been a network of other paths connecting each settlement or tribal area. The two main trackways may have formed a major east to west trade route across Southern England, though it is hard to be sure how much long-distance trade took place in prehistoric times. Over long periods of time it was probably travelled by many new peoples, bringing new ideas and ways of life.

When one looks for a similar route along the Greensand ridge, however, there is none. It was not as continuous a geographical formation as the North Downs, was naturally more densely covered with vegetation, was prone to slumping, and was less useful as an economic resource. There were also no spring line villages as at the base of the Downs. Sevenoaks however was peripheral to all of this; its north-south aligned ridge would have its day in times to come when a long distance north-south route would become important.

The great Neolithic stone monuments appeared at this time in the Medway Valley, from Trottiscliffe eastwards, and were clearly the work of an organised tribal society focusing on the Medway with an agricultural surplus which

2 The chalk pit at Polhill, that familiar white gash on the North Downs visible from Sevenoaks, seen here in the 1920s. Some of the beehive-shaped lime burning kilns can just be seen in the background.

allowed people the time to build such structures. There is no evidence that Holmesdale was part of this, although the possible re-use of sarsen stones in the wall of Otford church, and the existence of a peaked stone indicated by the place name of Copstone in Otford are suggestive.

The Bronze Age began around 1900 B.C. with the arrival from the now separated continent of the Beaker People. They are named for their distinctive pottery, and brought with them knowledge of the use of copper and later bronze. Bronze-Age metalworkers are thought to have travelled between settlements, bringing their raw materials and tools and the secrets of their craft with them. The bronze chisel found near Castle Farm, Shoreham and axe head from Donnington Manor, Dunton Green, may either have been locally made, or have come to the area through trade or capture.

Burial barrows, perhaps of local chieftains or members of important families, have been found at Millpond Wood in Greatness and at Otford Mount on the hills above Otford. At Greenhill Road in Otford a mid-Bronze-Age cremation urn was found containing bone fragments of a 30-year-old man. This almost certainly had a barrow over it once, and together with earlier finds on the upper slopes of Greenhill emphasises it as a well-placed strategic site, at the junction of two valleys.

The Celtic field, a small square field between a quarter and one hectare in size, originated at this time with the introduction of a new type of plough. These fields were ploughed in both directions to break up the soil, and were marked by low banks or lynchets at their margins. Lynchets from an Iron-Age field survive at Lullingstone, where they clearly were not superseded by the rectangular Roman strip fields.

The Iron Age, from 550 B.C. on, was marked by new waves of arrivals from the Continent, the consequence of first Greek and then Roman expansion in Europe. They brought iron tools, and later new forms of social organisation. The final group, the Belgae, were already part-Romanised when they arrived in 150 B.C. The growth of the network of hillforts in the Iron Age indicates more violent times. Warfare had brought many of the weaponry advances since late Mesolithic times and resulted from new

3 Chipstead's brickworks, photographed in the 1880s, was to the west of the village. Here the gault clay of the valley floor is fed into a hopper at top right, and the resulting extrusion is then cut to shape, under an improvised roof of thatch and sacking. On the far left appears to be part of a clamp where the bricks are fired. The village's *Brickmakers Arms* pub records this lost industry.

population pressures and competition for resources. These hillforts are naturally occurring well-defended sites, augmented by man-made ditches and fortified gateways. Oldbury Hill is one of the largest in the country, and had the tremendous advantage of an on-site spring. Hillforts at Hulberry, above Lullingstone, and at Squerryes Park, near Westerham are contemporary with Oldbury, and Otford Mount is another possible site.

The absence of evidence of settlement within these hillforts, even at Oldbury which contained 50 hectares within its ramparts, suggests their occupation by small warrior élites only. They would have commanded sustainable local territories. Danes Trench, a 700m. long ditch found on the 120m. contour at Polhill, is possibly the western boundary of a territory based on Otford Mount. Its northern boundary with Hulberry hillfort is thought to align with the Otford-Shoreham parish boundary, marked by a 1,000-year-old hedge, and its eastern boundary with Oldbury may be the Childsbridge Lane 'hollow way'.

These hillforts may have functioned partly as local ceremonial and trade centres for their hinterland, and also to control access both to the Medway river crossings and into the Weald. Oldbury, whose geology provides firmer ground to the south, effectively guards access to the Medway near Tonbridge whereas routes south via Sevenoaks ridge, while certainly in existence as droveways and hunting tracks, may have led to less fordable Medway crossings where the river was unbraided or had swampy margins.

The Weald with its heavy sticky clays was a difficult land to cross. Its name comes from Andredswald, the great forest feared by Julius Caesar, and called by the Venerable Bede 'thick and inaccessible, the abode of deer, swine and wolves'. It tended to be wooded, particularly with oaks, because there was no reason for anyone to clear it. Its iron supplies, though, were essential to the Iron-Age settlers for tools that allowed greater land clearance for agriculture, more permanent structures and settlements, more sophisticated crafts, and better weapons. In summer, the woodland tracks became passable again, and herders would take their pigs south into the Weald to feed on the acorns and beech mast in a pattern of life that had started in Mesolithic times and would continue into the medieval period. This has left numerous north-south running roadways in West Kent, and a pattern of land division that survives today. Parishes tend to run north-south, some still following the ancient boundaries which allowed tribal groupings to share the same mixture of resources. Each would have had a section of North Downs chalkland, a section of Darent Valley, and section of Greensand ridge woodland, and a section of Wealden forest: a good recipe for living in harmony with one's neighbours.

Ancient trackways, tribal boundaries and even individual fields survive today, where settlements have failed to do so. A rare survival is the Iron-Age farm site near Farningham which shows the typical small semi-oval ditched animal enclosure about 0.2 ha. in area, four causewayed entrances, a 5m. diameter hut site, and numerous storage pits. The timber round hut has been shown to be a relatively long lived structure, yet which could

be erected by a single man, assisted perhaps by a child. Traces of two others have been found in Lullingstone Park.

Caesar's expeditions to Britain in 55 and 54 B.C. and the Claudian invasion in A.D. 43 were prompted greatly by the desire for Cornish tin and Wealden iron. It is possible that the invading Claudian legions travelled along the North Downs trackways and passed along the Holmesdale valley after their landing at Richborough and their victory at the Medway crossing. The major Roman road across Kent, Watling Street (nowadays followed closely by the route of the A2), had no precursor and certainly the going would have been easier along the ancient routes under the Downs. At some stage, Oldbury hillfort may have been overwhelmed and there is evidence that a wooden gateway was burned, perhaps during an attack.

Roman influence would soon be felt in the valley, and by the next century there was a string of villas along the river Darent. Roman building remains have been found at Kemsing, Otford, Shoreham, Lullingstone, Eynsford, and Farningham, at a spacing of about 1.5 to 3 km., roughly

4   Seal Hollow Road, formerly called Locks Bottom Road, has changed very little since this early 20th-century picture. Its origins as a post-Ice-Age river valley are evident in its narrowness, accentuated by the early 19th-century Knole Park wall built by Welsh stonemasons.

equivalent to that of the later medieval villages. The river was an important trade link, and was navigable at least as far as Lullingstone.

The Roman villa acted in much the same way as the later medieval manor, as a centre for rural production, whose surplus could then be traded on a wider network. In the process tribal society was greatly altered. Tribal leaders became the equivalent of the rural gentry, and most must have adopted Roman ways wholeheartedly. They lived in rectangular Roman houses, and adopted the complete package of Roman culture, while lesser clan members would have continued to live in traditional timber huts. It is unlikely that they moved far from their original homes, and an indication of earlier Iron-Age settlements may be inferred from the villa distribution. The absence of occupation evidence for the Sevenoaks ridge is telling, though isolated woodlanders' huts would have left few traces.

The Roman villa was typically single storied in Britain, an array of rooms linked by an external corridor or verandah, which would grow by adding wings. These wings may even have housed separate family groups within an extended family unit, or have grown through subdivision on inheritance by several children, as is thought to have happened at Darenth. The pattern of corridor or verandah circulation is one that we associate with post-medieval housing and the need for privacy, in contrast to the more communal indigenous lifestyle.

In a 12 sq. km. area around Otford nine Roman structures have been found, five of which are villas or probable villas. The earliest, dating from the first century A.D., did not have the range of amenities of later villas or later rebuildings, which would include hypocaust heating, mosaic floors, painted plaster decoration, baths and shrines.

The 'Progress' villa, off the present-day Pilgrims' Way East in Otford, was typical. Built in the first century A.D. for a senior British tribal figure and replacing an earlier round hut, it followed the new Roman rectilinear form, having a string of rooms about 20m. long linked by an external south-west facing verandah. The base walls were of mortared flint probably up to a low cill, with a timber framed structure above, the flint base ensuring the survival of traces to the present day. The infill between the timber up-

rights would have been very similar to the hazel wattle and clay and dung daub of medieval times. Roofing was generally of straw or reed thatch, with clay tiles reserved for more prominent buildings. The clay tiles which have been found at Lullingstone are flat with two raised side edges, over which semi-circular weathering tiles would be set running down the roof slope, a clever arrangement if properly maintained.

The Progress villa was essentially a farm house and had a walled enclosure, the farmyard, to the rear of the house. A small kiln uphill from the villa may have been for pottery manufacture or corn drying, thus completing the complex. Some villas also had a smaller family courtyard, such as that suggested by the wings at Farningham's Roman villa, which was sited by the river 250m. south of the present mill.

'Progress' had a chequered life. The house was burned down around the year A.D. 200, possibly at the same time that Lullingstone's villa shows abandonment, perhaps due to the period of violent political unrest in Britain, which it seems must have reached into Holmesdale. The farmyard continued to be used during the next two centuries in the time-honoured practice that does not respect buildings but does respect estates. It is likely, however, that the house was rebuilt. A fragment of painted plaster has been found showing a man holding a spear, with a fragment of descriptive text from the *Aeneid* alongside. The quality of this work is thought to be of the fourth century, perhaps at the same time that Lullingstone's wonderful mosaic floors were being laid.

Other villa sites in Otford have been identified from tile and brick debris at Wickham Field (at the west end of modern Otford) which is near a spring, and in a field south east of the parish church. Further structures around Otford included a riverside hut at Lower Barn, a wooden cattle shed used for 30 years in the second century at The Charne, and a possible settlement on top of Greenhill, suggesting continuity with prehistoric occupation there. Kemsing's villa site at Springhead may have also had a water mill, while Shoreham's villa was a relatively large one, with a frontage of about 35m.

There was also a Romano-British cemetery at The Charne or Frog Farm in Otford, used mainly in the second century A.D. This had a polygonal

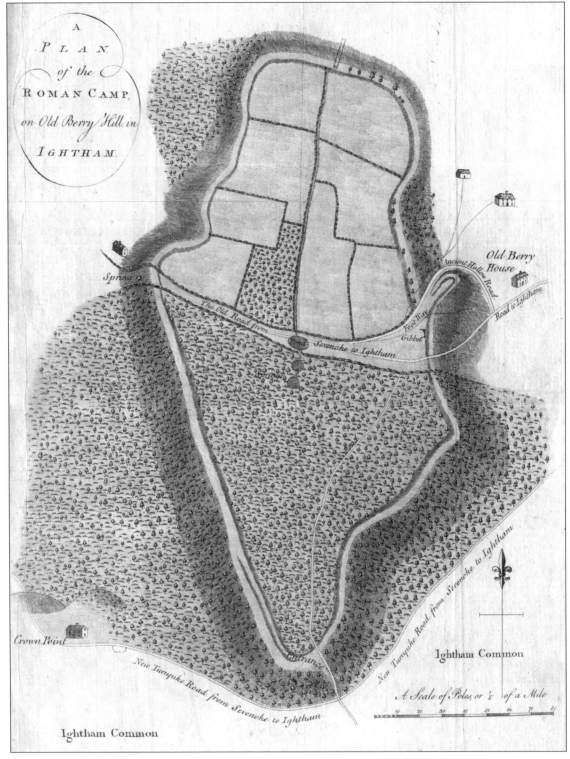

5   A map of Oldbury Hill, made soon after the 1765 turnpike when the old road was still usable, shows an even earlier 'hollow road'. The great size of the hill fort is clear, and the gibbet a reminder of the dangers of such out of the way areas.

6 Lullingstone Roman Villa's fourth-century mosaic floor showing Europa and the bull and, beyond, Bellerophon on Pegasus killing the Chimaera. The latter are surrounded by dolphins and representations of the seasons in a field of geometric patterns.

stone building about 6.5m. in diameter, which was possibly a mausoleum. The 74 grave groups over a 70-year period, together with other groups of graves in Ightham and Seal, suggest a large local population. The cemetery locations would have followed Roman tradition in being outside settlement boundaries and beside a road.

The Roman villa at Lullingstone was, however, the most important in Holmesdale and its development has parallels with that of medieval and later settlements and houses in the area, showing periods of growth and decline, and the technological and artistic advances that prosperity can bring. It was built around A.D. 80 for a Romano-British family, but differs from other local villas in having quite a deep plan, 15m. by 22m. overall width, facing east. Its plan includes a rear corridor and a front verandah between two short projecting wings, suggesting a pattern more like Farningham. The principal family rooms were in this original block, and there was a small enclosed court on the south side. To this complex a small circular temple would be added at the

beginning of the next century, with flint walls and a thatched roof.

Around the year A.D. 180 a Roman official, possibly a local governor, came to live here and added hot and cold plunge baths with a furnace on the south end, despite the fire risk. The kitchen behind the house was detached, as was more usual, and was dedicated with the ritual burial of an infant in a chalk hollow under the floor.

The spring-fed baths were partly buried into the ground and the heated section incorporated hypocaustic underfloor heating. The concrete floor and its mosaic covering was carried on square brick pillars or *pilae* creating a floor void through which warm air was ducted from a furnace room.

The religious cult rooms on the north side were also partly buried, and linked to a converted grain store, called by excavators 'the Deep Room', under the original house. A chalk lined pit in the middle of the floor held spring water, and a niche was painted with a fresco of water nymphs, perhaps a Romanised representation of indigenous naturalistic deities.

The villa was abandoned and left derelict between A.D. 200 and 280, though the detached kitchen block continued in use as a tannery, until a new Romano-British family reoccupied the villa at the close of the third century, during the unsettled times of Admiral Carausius's rebellion. They rebuilt and repaired the house, and the Deep Room became a shrine to their household gods, which they personified using the relocated marble busts left by the previous owner. A large granary was also built to the north of the house, with drying chambers: openings in the end walls ducted air through underneath slatted floors, an arrangement reminiscent of later oast houses. Its location by the river suggests larger scale farming by the new family, with river-borne exporting of grain to markets in London and beyond.

Around the year 300 a square temple or mausoleum was built. A timber-framed cloister surrounded an inner square chamber about 5m. wide built of chalk block walls with painted plaster and a red painted dome. Lead-coffined burials of a young man and woman were found here, on the site of the medieval church of St John the Baptist. In the second quarter of the fourth century the original part of the villa was extended and remarkable mosaic floors were laid in the new rooms, with Europa and her bull in one, and Bellerophon on Pegasus killing the Chimaera, surrounded by dolphins and personifications of the seasons, in the other. These sophisticated scenes on a field of geometric patterns were brought together with the vibrant roughness reminiscent of a medieval encaustic tile pavement.

The fourth century was a time when there were a great many religious beliefs and minority cults, and about A.D. 360 Christianity came to Lullingstone. The room above the Deep Room became a chapel, with frescos of early Christians at prayer and the Chi Rho symbol of Christ. There was no doubt some symbolism at work in the placing of the chapel above the pagan shrine, particularly since the latter continued to be used in parallel. There was a great difference, however, between the two. Pagan shrines were places where spirits and gods dwelt and were visited by individuals, unlike the communal worship of Christianity.

Within four decades, however, all activity on the site seems to cease, with the exception of Christian worship. The baths and then the granary were demolished, and finally a fire, perhaps in the early fifth century, consumed the remaining structure. Perhaps it was a matter of site clearance, or perhaps this burning was to discourage squatters and less civilised people, who seem to have occupied many deserted villas towards the end of their existence.

There is a general absence of dwelling remains for the ordinary people, the villa farm labourers, the new classes of specialists, manufacturers, builders and soldiers, the farmers of middle rank who had not yet achieved villa status or wealth, the inns and hostels for travellers in a more mobile world, and so on. The successors to the Iron-Age round hut were probably of equally limited life, arranged in small native settlements, with smaller groupings perhaps associated with the satellite villas, an arrangement that would recur locally in medieval times.

The greensand slopes of the future town of Sevenoaks were almost certainly wooded, the outer margins of the great Wealden forest, but still of economic importance to the Otford settlement. At its edge there was a small tile or brickworks at the future Bat and Ball refuse tip. Urn burials with cremated remains found at One Tree Hill on the Greensand ridge give an indication that there were tiny communities here, with tracks leading out to isolated pastures in the forest beyond. There were, however, no Roman roads into the Weald here, the nearest being that from Titsey to Edenbridge and beyond.

We do not know what part the upper Darent Valley played in its *pagus*, the administrative unit based on Rochester. This unit, which was revived by the Saxon Christian Church as a second diocese in the county, may have been a pre-existing subdivision, just as the new *civitates* were generally based on the Iron-Age tribal states.

The period of the Roman occupation was not as uniformly settled as at first appears. At least two of the villas in the valleys suffered damage around the year 200, a time of general economic depression, and later in that century raids by Franks, Saxons and the Irish, and a home-grown rebellion must have unsettled the valley's inhabitants; perhaps a presentiment of the final Roman withdrawal from Britain at the start of the fifth century.

II

The Renaming of the Landscape

The Saxon Settlements

The arrival of the Saxons is only directly recorded in the Anglo-Saxon Chronicle, written several centuries later, which tells of Hengist and Horsa being invited to the country to defend it from Pictish barbarian raiders, around the year A.D. 440. In the story, they are given the Isle of Thanet, at that time a true island, but some years later they drive the British armies of King Vortigern back across Kent, with decisive victories at the river crossings of Aylesford and Crayford. Hengist seizes the throne, while Horsa, possibly a representation of a horse god, dies, and the Britons flee to the west or are put to the sword.

In fact some Saxon immigration had begun a century before the Roman withdrawal, when mercenaries were hired by an overstretched administration. Evidence suggests some of these may even have been posted at Lullingstone, perhaps as guards. Within a decade of the withdrawal of the Roman legions in A.D. 410 more Saxons made their way into the west of Kent. The progress of their settlements up the river valleys of the Thames, Darent and Cray probably took place over an extended period as they arrived in small groups, either families, clans or whole villages.

The Saxons came to West Kent and the Thames Valley from their homelands in northern Germany looking for new lands. At the same time came other tribal groups such as the Jutes, who settled primarily in East Kent. The ethnic difference between the two halves of Kent coupled with their different landscapes and direction of early growth, led to a degree of

independence from the beginning, expressed later in the dual kingship of the Kingdom of Kent (the younger son ruling from Rochester and the older from Canterbury), in the twin sees of the early Christian Church, and in the surviving Man of Kent and Kentish Man distinction based on which side of the river Medway one is born.

The earliest arrivals in West Kent settled on the best agricultural land on the Thames coastal plain, and near the mouths of the Darent and Cray rivers. Later, the land further up the river valleys and the high downland and chartland would be exploited more, either by offshoot settlements or perhaps by new arrivals. The upper Darent was at some stage partitioned into river estates focused on very early settlements at Eynsford, Otford and Westerham. All three settlements have Roman and Iron-Age associations, which seems to have been an important factor in their early creation. Westerham was also a royal estate, both strategically important and, at 12,000 hectares, immense.

The earliest estates on the Thames coastal plain included most of the Downs, while early Holmesdale territories tended to start at the crest of the Downs and then extend south over the Chartland to the base of the Greensand scarp. The watershed was a natural dividing line, placing Knockholt in the Cray valley and Halstead in the Darent valley, a distinction perpetuated in later manorial and parochial subordinations. The choice of a settlement site involved a number of conscious or intuitive decisions by the new arrivals. The conflicting demands of access to water, and the need for a dry, well drained site, would have been among the most urgent site

7   Brasted Church, seen around 1900, is away from the main part of the village (once called Brasted Street). It is on a slight rise which must have reduced flooding, and is accompanied by the old school house.

8   Otford pond around 1905. The pond has been railed off in a gesture of civic tidiness.

choice characteristics. Kemsing, Chevening and Otford are spring-line villages, built on the lower flanks of the scarp of the North Downs, close to the ancient trackways, while Shoreham, Otford (again), Chipstead, Sundridge and Brasted are all riverside settlements where the availability of fish, power for milling, and the possibility of water transport must have more than made up for poorer water quality. These sites are more prone to flooding but, as the name Brasted suggests, the village was sited at a broad place, possibly a former river terrace, and may indicate that the choice of a small knoll for the church was a secondary factor.

Otford's church is located well to the east of the ford that gave the village its name. The original settlement may have been by this ford on a raised site, such as the former Roman site called The Charne, located above the water meadows to the west of the river. A burial has been found here, and an early Saxon pagan cemetery is further west at Polhill. The church's position, meanwhile, takes advantage of the junction of the Pilgrims' Way and the roadway down the valley to the north.

Before substantial churches were built, settlements were highly mobile: building in timber meant that rebuilding was easier than repair, and new structures could be completed before the old one was abandoned. The territory and its boundaries were of much greater importance than the actual siting of the dwellings and settlement.

Burials can supply the earliest evidence for Saxon settlement in the valley. In addition to individual burials, roadworks at Polhill in Victorian and more recent times have uncovered a cemetery of perhaps 150 to 200 graves in total. The hillside location was pagan and some burials had pagan elements, such as grave goods, weapons and clothes. They were not a very prosperous group, *ceorls* or freemen and small landowners, with an average life expectancy of 24 years. Whole families seem to be represented here – all the dead of a community which may have been the original Otford settlement by the river crossing. A small hut found in one corner of the compound may have had some ceremonial use, or may have housed a guard. Some later burials were Christian, showing the characteristic east–west grave alignment, and date the cemetery to between A.D. 650 and 750. It was probably

9 One of the early burials from the Saxon settlement of Otford found at the Polhill Cemetery.

abandoned when Shoreham church began to allow or encourage burials in its churchyard.

After the Romans left, little is know about the fate of the British. The Anglo-Saxon Chronicle records a bloody end to them, with survivors pushed ever westwards, yet the story of Hengist and Horsa peacefully co-existing with their British hosts for several years suggests no strong racial antipathy. That the Saxons called themselves the *Cantware*, the people of Kent, is suggestive, for the name comes from the Roman region *Cantium*, itself based on an earlier Celtic word meaning the rim of a bowl, a good metaphor for Kent's geographic position.

Perhaps after the battle of Aylesford the newcomers had become masters. The Saxon name for Britons is *wealh* as in the modern 'Welsh', but is also translated as 'slave'. As a place name it is found more in Surrey, as at Wallington. The British may have been left with the poorer, more marginal land, up on the Downs or on the Chartland slopes, while the Saxon settlers took the best land along the Holmesdale valley floor.

At one time it was thought that the Saxons avoided Roman sites. In fact they seem to have taken over the Roman fields and lived within the same land boundaries. Their settlements too were very close to local Roman villa sites, but they do not seem to have reoccupied the villas themselves; many of them were already in a poor state by the beginning of the fifth century, and repairing stonework, or a hypocaust floor, would have utterly defeated the Saxons. They built in timber,

10   Chevening, around 1930, is an archetypal estate village with its orderly row of retainers' cottages. The oldest cottage, central in the picture, is late 17th-century.

leaving less certain traces of their earliest settlements.

How then does one trace the settlement history of a people who built in wood and left few written records? One way is by the study of place names. The Saxons very thoroughly renamed the whole landscape, in a way that is similar to the American colonists' renaming of their continent. Both are cases of wholesale immigration, which contrast with the Normans' importation of the ruling class alone.

Very few names which originated before this Saxon immigration survived. Exceptions are the river names, which perhaps were long known to the seafaring Saxons through trade. The Celtic, or pre-Roman, name Darent means the water where oaks are plentiful, the first element of which is also found in the river Dour and its settlement Dover. An awareness of these earlier inhabitants is recorded in the name Oldbury, or old *burgh* or stronghold, and Hulberry (Lullingstone), stronghold in a wood.

Some of the earliest place names are those ending in '-ing' and '-ham'. The former means the people or descendants of, typically, a particular individual and is often associated with very

early spring settlements in Kent, thus Kemsing means Cymesa's people.

Chevening means the people of the ridge. The first syllable, originally *cefn*, is one of the very rare Celtic place name survivals, suggesting that the name was given by or to a British family group who continued to live alongside their Saxon neighbours.

The suffix 'ham' is often translated as farmstead or settlement, and comes from the same root as the word 'home'. Westerham is the western settlement, indicating an ancient boundary status, while Shoreham is the *ham* at the steep slope. Nearby Sepham is Seppa's *ham*; further downstream, at Farningham, the fern-dwellers had settled, while at Yaldham, near Seal, an old man or chieftain lived.

Tun, meaning farmstead, is also found in the word town, and in a sense a *tun* might be the seed from which a town would grow. In the Darent valley they have grown no larger than manors, as at Filston and Preston, near Shoreham, and at Kippington in Sevenoaks. It was possibly at Preston (priest's farmstead), that the position of the church and subsequent village at Shoreham was planned.

11   The much rebuilt medieval bridge at Shoreham was adjacent to an early ford.

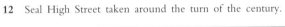

12   Seal High Street taken around the turn of the century.

Wickham, at the west end of Otford, may be a very early farm. The *wic* element appears to be derived from the Latin *vicus* or farm, and is often found in early Saxon towns. Proximity to a navigable river to allow long distance trade is a common element, and may have been another function of Wickham.

Roman influence is recorded in some 'stone' name endings. The Saxons would use this both for villa sites and paved roads. Lullingstone falls into this category and Stone Street may refer to a Roman road to Plaxtol which would have still been usable in Saxon times. Others, such as Chiddingstone, refer to stone outcrops and boundary markers, or are derived from *tun*. Copstone, near Otford, means peaked stone, and may refer to some Roman feature or even an earlier megalith.

The '-stead' suffix is translated as 'place', and is particularly associated with Downland stockfarms as at Halstead. Often on poorer soil they were secondary settlements, but perhaps Brasted, and to a lesser extent Chipstead, are unusual in being on the more fertile lands of Holmesdale, which has allowed them to grow much larger than their Downland namesakes. Rumstead, near Underriver, shows this process continuing into the Chartland and to the very edge of the Weald. 'Stow', rare in Holmesdale, has a similar meaning, and thus Plegstow in Twitton is a 'play place', which, like Plaxtol, may have seen some form of religious play or mystery acted out.

Early buildings are sometimes recorded in place names. The 'hall' at Seal may have been the ancestor of the manor of Seal and Kemsing,

13 Knockholt Church sketched in 1801 by W. Hemper before heavy Victorian alterations. The Norman windows are visible and in the churchyard are the once common timber grave-boards.

as power shifted from Kemsing to its daughter settlement of Seal, on the main road to Maidstone. In a similar vein, the later medieval manor of Blackhall, at the north-east end of Sevenoaks, was clearly a hall built of dark timbers. A cruder dwelling or 'bower' existed at Bore Place, in the Weald, while Nizels was memorable at one time for its new buildings.

Coldharbour is a common medieval place name, found near Penshurst and at Bessels Green, and may be an ironic reference to the local microclimate. It may also indicate a wayside shelter for travellers, as at Bessels Green on the Rye road.

Sundridge's name means 'sundered enclosure', the sundering or separating perhaps referring to its beginnings as a camp on the drove road to Somerden, near Chiddingstone, which was the summer pasture of Lewisham, Woolwich and Greenwich herdsmen. Another type of farm enclosure is recorded by the 'stall' element of Dunstall, to the east of Shoreham. 'Hatch', usually translated as gate, marks the edge of the common at Ivy Hatch, where probably the gateway was more metaphorical. Hills were distinctive features used to describe places, as recorded in names like Knole, or hillock, and Dunton Green, the 'ton' by the North Downs. Underriver translates as 'under the hill', while Riverhill, first recorded in 1258, is 'hill-hill'.

Often the original vegetation is named, or distinctive trees such as a group of oak trees at Sevenoaks, or an outlying oak thicket at Knockholt. Bitchet Green takes its name from some birch trees, perhaps some early regeneration after a storm. Twitton, meaning wood shavings, was the name given to woodland on the parish boundary between Otford and Shoreham which was presumably being managed for some economic reason.

Meanwhile in the Weald, whose name itself comes from the Saxon *wald* meaning wood, large groups of trees predominate. 'Hurst' is a very common name ending here, meaning a wooded hill, perhaps even one that becomes prominent through clearance around it. Penshurst seems to be a wooded hill within an enclosure or pen, but *pen* may be a dialect form of the Celtic *cenn* meaning a hill or head. Hursts are not confined to the Weald, however, as Great Cockerhurst, an

14 A more verdant Penshurst village and church in the days before the motor car. The influence of the architect Devey can be seen in the decorative chimney-stack to the left of the picture.

ancient farm near Shoreham, shows. In the Weald clearings for pasture, such as at Leigh, become noteworthy, and in this case are so unusual that the more descriptive prefix is dispensed with.

'Dens', or woodland valley pastures, were settled when temporary camps were built here by herdsmen bringing their pigs for fattening on the acorns and beechmast, and gradually became more permanent farmsteads in their own right, and then villages and towns. 'Den' is the most common settlement name in the Kentish Weald, but can also be found on the Chartland around it, as at Dibden on the western edge of Sevenoaks. Shenden (on the Tonbridge Road south of Sevenoaks), however, appears to be derived from *dene*, and may mean holy valley, although no religious connection is known.

'Chart', which first appears in the seventh and eighth centuries, denotes the stony heathland found on the lower Greensand, as at Brasted Chart and Seal Chart. The impression given is of large treeless areas, covered with gorse, broom and bracken, but as woodland tends to re-establish itself this suggests very early clearance.

The importance of water is shown in many names, such as Childsbridge ('child' meaning a spring), and Solefields, from *sole* meaning a muddy pool built for animals. Safe and firm-bottomed river crossings often gave rise to settlements, as at Eynsford (Aegen's ford), Otford (Otta's ford) and Longford at Dunton Green. A settlement by a ford makes the most fertile soil on both sides of a river equally accessible, and also strategically locates itself on the two most important communication routes (along and across the river). Most of the Darent valley settlements are at river fords, but the early pre-eminence of Otford and Eynsford, combined with the 'ford' suffix in their names, suggests that at one time they may have been the only ones, giving their owners, Aegen and Otta, considerable power.

Less obvious water names are found in the valley, as at Riverhead, meaning cattle landing place. The second element is derived from *hythe*, a name more familiar in coastal or estuarine locations. The stream rising in Montreal Park is culverted under the road these days, and it seems hard to believe that it was once navigable from here to the sea. Rye, near Dunton Green, means 'at the island', while Noah's Ark, near Kemsing, is a more recent name with the same theme, referring to raised ground where animals would herd themselves together during floods.

Early Saxon society in West Kent was, in theory at least, a very free one, a community of freeholders each owing allegiance to the King alone. This was a frontier society too, with a greater degree of personal freedom at the advancing edge of the cleared and cultivated lands, a pattern that would persist as the frontier moved up into the Downlands and Chartlands and then out into the Weald.

Westerham was unusual in extending much further into the Weald, a legacy of its early royal ownership (since the Weald was royal owned

woodland or *snoad*). By the eighth century those in the original lands of North Kent as well as Holmesdale exercised rights over the resources of the Weald. Bexley, for example, had dens in Hever mixed in with those of Plumstead, Orpington and Brasted. Brasted's dens were strung out in a line along the drove road to Hever and Edenbridge, while Otford's more scattered dens resulted from an earlier sharing of a large common amongst the Archbishop's submanors. The manor of Penshurst Halimote, which included the village but not Penshurst Place, was still known as Otford Weald in the late 18th century, much as Sevenoaks Weald retains its subordinate name today.

There was an early Saxon settlement at Lullingstone, near the former Roman villa. One can imagine approaching it from the edge of the cultivated land: first, the stock fences, perhaps some repaired Roman or Celtic earth embankments, then an apparently random arrangement

15   The valley of Shenden on the Tonbridge road south of Sevenoaks. Its name may mean 'holy valley' and across here in 1450 Cade's men would have chased the King's troops in the Battle of Solefields. In 1968 this was the site of the colourful Turner's Nurseries, but is now built over.

16 The copper-spired Riverhead Church around 1890. The part-ragstone house to the south may once have been an inn, having cellars as well as a large courtyard behind. It was later a stonemason's yard, masons' marks surviving on a wall behind the present-day Memorial Hall, while in the house was a school run by the mason's daughter, tuition costing 2d. a week. The building was demolished for road widening.

of timber huts roofed in local river reeds with well-trodden muddy paths winding between. Some huts have vertical plank walls, consisting of two staggered layers of regular cut and adzed boarding, fixed together with pegs, and with gaps caulked with mud. These are the noisy family homes and smoke filters through their roofs and out of open windows. Other, smaller huts are buried up to their roof eaves in the ground, and within, the floor is sunken and the walls are bare earth. These are the craft buildings and one catches a glimpse of a loom inside one. Near the centre of the village, there is a more substantial hut, the village chieftain's, and all around there are animals, particularly pigs.

Meanwhile Otford was becoming the administrative centre of this part of the valley, and its neighbour Shoreham the ecclesiastical centre in the centuries that followed St Augustine's landing and conversion of King Ethelbert of Kent to Christianity in A.D. 597. Otford's strategic position is easier to understand. It is on the Green Way, and is fairly centrally located between the western and eastern arms of Holmesdale and the river valley to the north. The settlement also looks to the south, towards the bulk of its territory up the Chartland slopes and beyond to the Weald. Between Otford and Shoreham there is a low spur, a remnant of the once continuous chalk face of the Downs. Shoreham nestles up against this and the view from the church is thereby funnelled down the valley towards the north, towards the mother church and original settlement. The early 'mother' churches, or minsters, were communities of priests who went out into the surrounding countryside to preach in the open air. Preston ('priest's *tun*') may have been their home, though it is more likely that it was a farm granted to them for their support.

The original minster church in Shoreham was probably roughly in its present position. However, the earliest remains found to date are of a

17 Eynsford's bridge and ford, with the close-studded
Plough Inn across the river, and, just visible at the right,
the barrel-roofed mill.

simple early Norman two-cell church which starts
at the present-day church's west wall, and con-
sists of a rectangular nave with a much smaller
chancel at the east end. Many earlier Saxon timber churches are thought to have been rebuilt by
the Normans in stone. Evidence of the pre-
Conquest origin of most local churches is given
within part of the *Textus Roffensis*, written during
the winter of 1122–3 or earlier. This lists churches
paying for chrism oil, and is almost certainly a
copy of an earlier Saxon list.

   The list includes, in no particular order,
Pennesherst (Penshurst), Ehteham (Ightham),
Lullingestuna (St Botolphs, Lullingstone),
Lullingestana (St John the Baptist, Lullingstone),
Westerham, Watlande (Woodlands), Ciullinga
(Chevening), Aeinesford (Eynsford), Cimisinga
(Kemsing), Sela (Seal), Bradesteda (Brasted),
Faeringeham (Farningham), Sunderersce
(Sundridge), Mapledreskampe (Maplescombe),
Scorham (Shoreham), Otteford (Otford),
Cidingstane (Chiddingstone), Haltested (Halstead),
Gretenersce (Greatness), Seounaca (Sevenoaks),
and Sciburna (Shipbourne). In other words vir-
tually every pre-19th-century church in the area,

18 Filston Hall's medieval moated site predates the
present 17th-century house.

19 A reconstructed early Saxon hut at West Stow shows the likely form of house and earliest church construction in Holmesdale. The vertical double layers of planks would have been very prone to rot, and must be the major reason for the absence of any surviving structures.

including several that no longer exist. Shoreham, dating from the late seventh or early eighth century was the earliest religious foundation in the valley. A grant of land at Milton (the middle 'ton') in 821 by Cedwulf of Mercia to the Archbishop of Canterbury is thought to refer to Shoreham.

Shoreham's minster status is shown by the number of churches over which it retained authority, even into the Middle Ages when Shoreham was a deanery with 34 churches under its control. It also retained a larger parish than most of its subordinates. Kemsing, Eynsford and Westerham were other mother churches with almost minster status. Kemsing spawned and had control over Seal church, Eynsford over Farningham and the two Lullingstone churches, and Westerham over Edenbridge.

A further stage is represented by Chevening and Brasted churches, the latter being a known daughter church of Shoreham. These themselves later become the mother churches of Sundridge, Chiddingstone and Hever churches, but they never attained minster status. Brasted and Hever seem to have been carved out of Westerham and Sundridge from Chevening in such a way as to give long thin parishes which, reflecting the secular estates, extend from the Downs watershed to the base of the Greensand ridge. This pattern was not repeated when Seal was formed, as Seal is directly south of Kemsing; instead, Kemsing's parish extends almost up to Seal Church, and Seal then extends up the chartlands to its south.

A lesser and later class of the daughter churches of Shoreham includes Otford, Sevenoaks, Halstead, Woodlands and Penshurst. They may have begun as chapels which later gained parochial rights, but some chapels never made this transition, including St John the Baptist at Greatness (later refounded as a hospital), Chapel Wood near Seal, the well-side chapels in Kemsing and Otford, and private manorial chapels of medieval and later date including Knole, Bradbourne, Brook Place (Riverhead), St Clere (Kemsing), Cory Yokes (Knockholt) and Preston (Shoreham).

St Nicholas Church in Sevenoaks probably originated as a wayside shrine or *crouch* along Otford's drove road, as did the chapel of St John the Baptist to the north. Both are frequent wilderness dedications in Kent, St Nicholas also being the patron saint of mariners. Nothing remains of the early crouches or timber crosses which marked wayside shrines. There was one on the drove road half a mile south-east of Chevening, one at Tanners Cross to the east of Seal, one at Sevenoaks market place (the market cross), one perhaps at Cross Keys near Dibden, and one called Oaks Cross at the base of the Greensand scarp on the drove road from Seal. Stone Cross, near Seal, may have been a medieval development of the crouch, but nothing remains today.

Kemsing's status as an early church is shown by its unusual dedication to St Mary and St Edith. St Edith is said to have been born at a small convent or royal house in Kemsing in 961. Her mother appears to have been an unwilling bride of King Edgar's who quickly retired to Wilton Abbey with Edith, each becoming Abbess in due course. Following Edith's early death at 23, miracles were ascribed to her, which led to her canonisation. The story raises some questions, such as why Edith was born at Kemsing, and whether such a nunnery did exist. A religious house in Kemsing is not out of the question, given the church's quasi-minster status, and local tradition locates it at the site of the present-day Box House. The linkage of St Edith with the well in the centre of Kemsing almost certainly was made long after the spring was first used.

Holy wells became particularly popular in the early medieval period although their use certainly predates that time. They are typically associated

20   St Nicholas' Church and the Upper High Street, Sevenoaks, in traffic-free earlier times.

with female saints, as at Kemsing, which may be a continuation of the Celtic female water spirit cults. Pre-Christian fertility practices were continued into the Middle Ages at St Edith's well, which was used to bless the harvest, and the cult of St Bartholomew at Otford, said to assist in human fertility. St Thomas's Well in Otford, meanwhile, is said to have been created by Archbishop Thomas Becket striking the ground. Water is said to have issued forth, yet this was the same water source which was used by the nearby Roman villa. The waters here were used until the early years of this century to treat children's grazes, as were the waters of St Edith's well for bad eyes. Holywell Shaw on the Westerham-Brasted boundary marks another spring renowned in the Middle Ages for curative properties, and the chapel and later hospital of St John the Baptist at Greatness may have come into being be-

cause of nearby medicinal springs. The well on Church Field near Riverhill may also have had holy status, linked with the local tradition that St Julian had a home nearby. Local place names, such as St Julian's, Holy Field and Church Field are very suggestive and occasional shaped stones have been found around Rumstead which may have been part of a wayside rest house dedicated to him. The hillslope is prone to landslip which may have destroyed or concealed such a building.

Some of the earliest churches were built at previously pagan sites. Celtic religion was very naturalistic, including worship at sacred trees and groves, healing springs and wells, ponds and stones, and high places. Augustine's new Christian church was instructed to build on this tradition in a very physical sense, even using trees from the groves to provide the timber for the new churches. Some churchyard yew trees have been found to be over

21 St Edith's well in Kemsing (photographed *c.*1875), with its ragstone surround, locally held to have been built from the ruins of the 12th-century castle.

2,000 years old, making them already old when the first church was built beside them. Kemsing lost a 1,300-year-old yew tree in 1921, which had been growing in front of the chancel. Church-yard yews may have been favoured and spared because of their symbolic links with eternal life and Christ's blood. Indeed the position of the church may have been chosen because of these trees, and perhaps other pagan associations of the site.

The Saxons divided Kent into seven lathes. The western-most, which included Holmesdale, is that of Sutton-at-Hone (the south 'ton' of Dartford). This system of subdivision dates back to the earliest Saxon and Jutish settlement in the county and may be based on the natural differences in the county's landscape. The lathe was an administrative unit for collecting taxes and administering justice. Later Westerham would

become part of the separate lathe of Wallington, which reflected some cross-border territorial ownership. Lathes were further subdivided in the tenth century when the hundredal system was introduced to Kent from Wessex. In part this was to give greater control for repelling the Viking invasions and raids, but it was also a natural consequence of an increased population and an in-creasingly stratified society.

The Hundred of Codsheath is unusual in the extent to which it reflects earlier estate and parish boundaries, something most of the other 66 Kentish hundreds ignore. It extends from Shoreham at the north to present-day Sevenoaks Weald, and from Sundridge in the west to Seal Chart in the east.

The Hundred in theory was composed of 10 tithings, a tithing being a collection of ten house-holders, each held responsible for the good conduct of the others. This was a very effective, although not particularly fair, method of self-policing. Tithings survived well into the Middle Ages, when members could be fined for not repairing a road and for concealing its true state (Shoreham Tithing 1406), and for failing to keep watch and thus catch a fugitive (Sepham Tithing 1414). In 1284 Sepham had a community of 12 households and perhaps 50 people.

The Hundred Court administered local customary law, including debts, trespass and inheritance fines. All householders had to attend the four-weekly court and would be fined for failure to do so, though, with the number of cases and the problems of bringing together all the parties, witnesses and juries, attendance was a heavy burden and many may have preferred to pay the fine. The courts were held in the open air and heaths were a preferred location. In the Middle Ages Codsheath's court was held on the hilltop behind Riverhead, though an alternative or earlier location has been suggested at the junction of the modern London and Otford roads, in the heart of Sevenoaks. The association of such a centre with both a pre-Conquest market and a convenient landmark, such as a group of seven trees, is known from other Hundreds. The name, Codsheath, also seems more plausible on the heathy Chartland. Its oldest known form, 'Godehede' of 1178, may mean 'God's Heath', a pagan holy place. The market in Sevenoaks is certainly pre-Conquest in origin and, though the name might suggest a pre-Christian ritual site at a grove of seven trees, its likeliest beginnings are during the stability of the mid-10th century after Danish invasions had ceased.

In early Saxon times the economy had largely been a subsistence one with limited local barter. Trade was controlled by the King and its benefits were passed on by him as gifts. Later, however, markets were encouraged by King Alfred and his successors who were keen to control and profit from them. They made transactions outside the market illegal, while coinage was developed and there followed a proliferation of mints, in reality approved coin makers in many growing towns. Many early markets were in boundary areas, profiting from the neutrality of the place and the freedom from control and tolls. If Otford had an early market, nothing is known of it. Sevenoaks's

market may have originated as a form of boundary market, while Westerham may have been a more regional market, being on a county boundary. The origins of Chipstead (first mentioned in 1191) are less clear. Its name means 'market place', and others of the same name are found in Surrey and Kent where typically they have no associated settlements. In the Middle Ages the fish route from Rye to London crossed the river Darent at Chipstead, before climbing the North Downs to Chevening. In Saxon times this north-south route did not exist, except as a possible linkage of Wealden drove tracks with iron workers' tracks along the Sussex border with Kent. What little traffic there may have been from Otford to London (London being a Mercian rather than Kentish town) would have taken a more direct route. If Chipstead was an early market this may have been due to its boundary position between Otford and Westerham.

Holmesdale was at the periphery of the early Kingdom of Kent, a backwoods area, less developed agriculturally and structurally. A massive earth bank 2km. west of Westerham straddles the present A25, marking the county boundary. This was a defensive ditch thrown up by the Kentings against a threat from the west, possibly the Suthrige, the warriors of Surrey in the fifth and sixth centuries.

The Kingdom, at one time the most powerful in the country, fell under the control of Mercia and later Wessex in the eighth century, with only brief periods of independence thereafter. The battle of Otford in 775 marks one of these, when King Offa of Mercia attempted to suppress a Kentish rebellion. The battle is thought to have taken place by the river, the men of Kent presumably choosing to confront the enemy at the crossing and on the marshy ground beside the river. It is not clear who won the battle, although Kent enjoyed a short period of freedom afterwards. Casualties were said to be high, and tradition holds that local incidences of tetanus are due to the mass graves of men and horses.

Ultimately, Mercian domination may have boded well for the future of Holmesdale. It is believed that Offa granted Otford to Christ Church, Canterbury in 790, perhaps to atone for having killed Christians in the battle 15 years before, thus beginning Otford's 750-year

22 The tradition of seven oak trees growing near the *White Hart Inn* on the south approach to the town (photographed before 1906), like those on the Vine, only goes back a couple of centuries. If there were seven original oaks, their likeliest location would have been in the town, perhaps near the future St Nicholas' Church.

23 Chipstead Square in the 1920s, with some popular event taking place in front of the village's ragstone almshouses. In the background, the sign of the *Crown* public house can be seen.

association with successive archbishops. Later Mercian rulers consolidated this with land grants in Shoreham, Otford, Kemsing, Seal and Greatness in 821 and 822, bounded on the south by Andred, the great Wealden forest, which then covered the whole of the Chartland.

The valley may have escaped from the worst excesses of the Danish invasions in the ninth and 10th centuries. Beginning in 832 these targeted the wealthy communities of the north and east Kent coastal lowlands. Hidden away and without obvious wealth, Holmesdale may have been saved, and ironically, placed in a far better position once stability returned in the mid-10th century. The Danes visited the valley in 1016, laden with plunder following an abortive siege of London by Canute. They were heading east, and perhaps descending the North Downs ridgeway at Polhill,

when Edmund Ironside intercepted them. This second Battle of Otford was more of a skirmish, its location marked by Polhill place names, such as Danes Field, Danes Bottom and Danes Trench. King Edmund, however, failed to complete the rout due to the treachery of a supposed ally at Aylesford, and Canute became king soon afterwards.

In two hundred years the Danes had changed from being the stuff of nightmares to becoming rulers of the Kingdom. England had greatly changed during this time. Kings and nobles had taken greater powers as a reward for the protection they offered. Greater obligations were imposed on the dependent, and were never relaxed when peace returned. It was the beginning of feudalism, a vertically stratified society, in place of the earlier, freer and more communal one.

III

The Market Economy

Norman and Medieval Sevenoaks

Local tradition has long held that Longford, the river crossing at present-day Dunton Green, saw both King Harold's and William of Normandy's armies pass by within several weeks of one another in 1066. Harold would have been hurrying down to his nemesis at Hastings after defeating the Vikings at Stamford Bridge, and then William would have passed through on his cautiously indirect approach to London, via Canterbury and Winchester.

William's route can certainly be traced 20 years later in Domesday Book by the loss of value of manors along the corridor followed by his army. This was thankfully not the awful destruction that he practised along the Sussex coast to entice Harold into battle, or later seen in his merciless 'harrying of the north'. It was more likely a natural consequence of a hungry, foraging army on the move. The path of devastation recorded is fairly narrow, with the manor of Seal and Kemsing being particularly affected, suggesting a lengthier

24 Otford green and its overgrown pond in the 19th century.

27

stay by the army there. This may coincide with an account of William's illness and recuperation at a place with a ruined tower, thought to be the manor of Otford. Otford, perhaps in consequence, seems to have suffered far less from William's passing.

On his journey through Kent William is said to have been met by the leaders of the Church at the Medway crossing, who blocked his path and demanded a continuation of the Kentish law and custom. He is said to have agreed, an unlikely outcome, yet somehow it did survive this transition of power and even became codified – a matter of some consequence in the development of the county.

It is usually held that the Normans established the feudal system, but it was more a continuation and formalisation of a trend that had begun in late Saxon times. The new King William seized, and held as absolute owner, all land in his new Kingdom. Some he administered directly, but most he passed on to tenants-in-chief in return for goods and services. Estates which had become fragmented through gavelkind in Saxon times were now consolidated.

These tenants-in-chief included the barons and knights who were with William on the battlefield at Hastings. His half-brother, the odious Odo, Bishop of Bayeux, accumulated many scattered holdings in the Kentish downlands. He took Seal and Kemsing from a Saxon nobleman, Brixi, and seized Sundridge, a former church possession which had been previously appropriated by Earl Godwin, King Harold's father. (Archbishop Lanfranc recovered Sundridge from Odo by the time of Domesday Book.) Count Eustace of Boulogne meanwhile received the manor of Westerham.

Church estates were typically handed back to the Church, as was the case with the manor at Otford, but with the addition of new feudal obligations. The Archbishop now had to provide knights for the King, and so had to assign lands in Sepham, Filston, Chevening and Halstead to knightly sub-tenants, in this case Haimo, Sheriff of Kent, Robert the Interpreter, and Geoffrey de Ros, who also held the surviving manor of Lullingstone from Bishop Odo. These tenants took over the Archbishop's feudal obligations and, over time, formed new sub-manors. Sepham even

became a small hamlet with about 10 houses, and was called the Half-Burgh (or half borough) of Upsepham in the 16th century. Brasted and Eynsford, and later Sundridge, were also assigned to the Archbishop's knights.

Later, the Archbishop surrendered much of his land in the western Weald to the Clares of the Lowy of Tonbridge, retaining only Penshurst Halimote, including the village, since it had farmable land. Tonbridge, and the London to Hastings route via Oldbury Hill, had become strategically important after the Conquest, and was given to William's trusted knight, Gilbert Clare, along with Wealden estates formed out of the Archbishop's Wrotham manor. The Clare family later came to control most of the western Weald, as well as obtaining in the 12th century the manors of Filston and Milton (Seal) with their attached dens in Chiddingstone, and inheriting Brasted with its dens near Hever.

Domesday Book of 1086 was commissioned by William to enable him to assess the extent of his new Kingdom. It is primarily a record of property values, and certain details, such as the existence of churches, are not always included.

The entry for Otford Manor records a total of 13 serfs, men who were effectively slaves, and who would sleep at night with the animals they herded or ploughed with during the day. There were 29 bordars, smallholders with holdings averaging eight acres, and 117 villeins or men of the village who had larger holdings. This gives an estimated total population of about 600 in an area which included Otford, Shoreham, Halstead, Chevening, Woodlands, Sevenoaks, Sevenoaks Weald and Penshurst. It was not a poor area and there were both fewer members of the lowest classes and larger than average land holdings. Other local manors had proportionally more serfs, particularly Brasted, where there were 15, in comparison to 24 villeins and 16 bordars. Brasted and Eynsford both had two mills, while Sundridge, recently separated from Otford, had three-and-a-half. This is a perplexing number of mills, but they were of comparatively low value, and were probably small or dilapidated.

Otford manor had six water mills to which tenants would have been obliged to take their corn, at Otford, Shoreham, Greatness, Longford, and Whitley, the sixth being a second mill at one

25 Otford Mill, in the background, was destroyed by fire in 1924.

of the settlements. Two other mills were held by knights, possibly at Chipstead and Bradbourne. Mills at all these places existed until recent times, and the remaining buildings at Otford, Greatness, Longford and Chipstead probably occupy their original locations. Whitley is an unusual place for a mill, for the area was one of the Archbishop's main timber reserves and probably sparsely populated, though it may have been chosen as being convenient for the emerging manors and growing market of Sevenoaks.

The complex pattern of submanors, tenancies and feudal obligations was due in part to *gavelkind*, the Kentish custom of partible inheritance, where the widow and all sons inherited in equal shares. The manor was in a sense a federation of scattered holdings rather than a unity, and was subject to many pressures. Sevenoaks, Shoreham and Sepham became separate manors very shortly after Domesday, while later manors were generally even more scattered, and Penshurst had holdings scattered over 35 square miles. The manor of Westerham retained control over its enormous domain by using an infield and less continously cultivated outfield system. It was given to Westminster Abbey by Edward I in 1290, following the death of his wife Queen Eleanor, and a chapel was built adjoining the mid-13th-century stone-built hall at Squerryes Lodge.

The manor was subdivided into yokes for ease of administration, the word 'yoke' being peculiarly Kentish, derived from the Roman unit of measurement, the *iugum*. Yoke sizes varied depending on the value of the land, an average area locally being around 200 acres. Of the 12 yokes of Shoreham in 1284, Sepham, Timberden and *Ecclesia* (Church) have recognisable names today. These yokes may have led to later villages and submanors or they may have been based on existing farms and settlements.

As holdings became fragmented through gavelkind, they became effectively unworkable. The freedom to alienate and dispose of holdings allowed families to elevate their status by enlarging and consolidating their lands, and while gavelkind tenure was not always completely free of feudal obligations, they tended to be lighter. Tenants' obligations were enforced by the manorial courts, known as Courts Baron, which were held every three weeks at Otford in the Court Hall. It was here that approval for land transfers would have been sought by rising local families; licences to marry were granted, rents delivered, fines for trespass and death duty paid, and breaches of manorial law or custom punished.

The suffix 'Court' in Kent often denotes the pre-eminent house, usually a domestic hall house, where courts were once held. Only a handful of court buildings are known to have been specifically built for the purpose. Ironically, Otford's Court Hall, which still exists in a much altered form to the west of the church, has been renamed The Chantry, suggesting a religious status that it never had. Its true function was identified by Anthony Stoyel from the very high quality of

26 Shoreham's paper mill on the River Darent.

27   The *Lamb Inn*, Sundridge, around 1900, faces a full mill pond (and mill in the distance) across the muddy road.

its large section oak timbers, which indicate a considerable investment. And yet the plainness and lack of ornamentation of these timbers contrasts with those of a rich merchant's house of the same age, around the year 1400. There was no soot blackening of the roof timbers, the normal indication of an open hall in which the smoke of an open fire would have risen up to a vent in the roof. It was therefore an unheated building from the outset, and could never have been intended as a dwelling.

The upper floor where the courts were held would have been a continuous room open to the roof, about 12m. long. At one end the archbishop's steward would have sat with his court officials, possibly on fixed benches against the wall. Despite its size, the room may not have been large enough for all the male tenants over 12 years of age (whose presence was mandatory), the participants in disputes and their witnesses. Some would have had to wait outside, sheltering under the partly open ground storey, beside store rooms and a lock-up for offenders. Before the Court Hall was built, courts were probably held

in the hall of the Archbishop's Manor House, the predecessor of the present ruined Palace, or outside the church gate, as at Penshurst.

The hundredal court, or Court Leet, dealt with the local administration of the borough, and civil and criminal cases, and continued to meet in the open at Codsheath, at its twice yearly law day. Justice was a rare commodity, particularly where powerful individuals were involved. In the 1330s, William Moraunt, of Morants Court and Henden Manor, was a Sheriff of Kent, and was in dispute with the Lyouns, occupants of a mill, possibly at Greatness. Moraunt seems to have got an accomplice to accuse John and Alice Lyoun of stealing a horse, for which John was hanged and Alice imprisoned. The conspiracy eventually came out, but Moraunt does not seem to have been brought to justice, and, in fact, his accomplice was later pardoned for his part in it.

The Church was the focus of village life in a strange mixture of sacred and secular. The earliest trading may have taken place in local churchyards, and bargains and agreements would be struck, tithes collected, and feasts riotously celebrated in them. The parish was symbolically centred on its church. The annual 'beating of the bounds' took place at rogationtide, just before Ascension Day, when the boundary markers were confirmed: sometimes the trees had died or the stones had been moved. The men went in a clockwise direction from the church, and often had a difficult journey where there were no tracks. Young boys were taken along, too, and were in some cases beaten at various boundary markers to guarantee an enduring, if painful, memory. This happened at Knockholt in 1822, where 63 boundary markers had to be verified, and the Vestry had allowed £1 for the food and drink for participants. At Otford 70 marks cut on oak, ash and beech trees had to be verified in the 1794 beating of the bounds.

The earliest surviving parts of Shoreham, Otford, Kemsing and Sevenoaks churches date from the 11th century, though at Otford there may be some very late Saxon fragments (a north wall including Roman quern stones and sarsen boulders, and rubble quoins of ironstone, flint, river bed calcareous tufa and reused Roman bricks) and at Kemsing there is a door which is possibly Saxon, and some herringbone walling. The semi-circular apse of Eynsford Church may also be from an original Saxon ground plan, or a stylistic link with its 12th-century owner, Christ Church Priory in Canterbury. Judging by entries in the *Textus Roffensis*, almost all medieval churches in Holmesdale had an earlier Saxon predecessor. They were probably built of timber, perhaps like that at Greenstead in Essex, which has walls of vertically-arranged split tree trunks. No traces whatsoever have been found to date, even at Sevenoaks where a major excavation has recently taken place. The focal position of the surviving churches, their unerring choice of the best site, suggests that later burials and foundations would have obliterated the post holes and shallow footings of the Saxon buildings.

The earliest version of the church at Sevenoaks dates from the immediate post-Conquest period. It was a simple Norman two-cell church, consisting of a nave and a smaller chancel, its position marked by the original columns at the west end of the nave, from which the present church has grown outwards in all four directions. Surprisingly it was larger than Shoreham's church

28   Otford's squat church, and to the right the medieval court hall (now a private house).

of the same period, but Shoreham's pre-eminence in the hierarchy of local churches cannot be questioned (in 1018 it had become a peculiar of the Archbishop of Canterbury), even if Sevenoaks was already asserting its status.

Little is known about the life of the local clergy in this period. Adam of Usk, the Rector of Kemsing in 1399, seems to have been an unconventional figure, taking part in student riots while at Oxford, later becoming a Doctor of Laws and a Member of Parliament, and practising occasional highway robbery. A later vicar of Seal, Thomas Theobald, carried out intelligence work on the continent for Henry VIII.

William de Shoreham, named after his birthplace, was a monk living around the year 1300, who has been called a great pre-Chaucerian poet. His work has touches of the absurd, and it is hard to tell how much of this was intentional. One poem sets out details of

29 Becket's well in Otford during excavations in 1953. The water conduit opening in the end wall and the stone pavement base are visible.

who can marry whom, a particular problem in small communities and, for example, tells us that a widow is allowed to marry the godfather of her stepchildren. Another poem advises that christening should only be carried out with water, and rules out wine, cider and beer in a strong Kentish dialect. Its success may have been due to the ambiguity that allowed it to be received as wisdom by some, and as humour by others.

Following the Conquest, William I encouraged the building of mottes, earthen mounds formed from the spoil of their surrounding circular ditches. Eynsford Castle began as a large low motte thrown up towards the end of the 11th century. A timber watch tower stood in the centre, surrounded by a thick flint wall. This was a large enough structure to be permanently occupied, and the first timber domestic structures, complete with *garderobe* toilets, took advantage of the existing wall and were built up against it. In the 12th century a stone hall,

complete with undercroft and solar, was built more centrally within the enclosure, using flint and reused Roman bricks.

Independent castles could be a threat to the monarch and royal assent was required for building – a measure often ignored during Stephen's reign (1135-54) and the civil war against Matilda (Henry I's daughter) when Shoreham and Kemsing castles were built. Shoreham Castle was in ruins by the 16th century and now only fragments survive in the walls of Castle Farm. It may originally have been on an island in the river channel, and the periodic meanderings of the river Darent have led it to swap banks in the last two centuries. Of Kemsing Castle nothing remains beyond a low raised area about 40m. across in the grounds of a private house, 'The Keep', to the north of the village centre. It may have been built of timber, with a palisade and timber buildings, similar to the first post-Conquest mottes, and was probably equally short-lived.

Matilda's son, Henry II, succeeded Stephen to the throne and brought a period of stability. Thomas Becket, his friend and Lord Chancellor, stayed at Otford during his brief tenure as Archbishop of Canterbury and is remembered for his irritation at being kept awake by nightingales, and for his creation of a water supply for his manor house by striking the ground with his staff. The latter has mythical overtones but may record the marking of a position on the ground by Becket or his steward, defining the position of the original conduit house, now called Becket's Well. The large rectangular stone tank, 10m. by 4m. by 2.5m. deep, which survives today is its late medieval successor, and would originally have been roofed. The holy status of the 'well' followed his martyrdom and is linked with the holy well cults of the mid-medieval period.

Becket's martyrdom was followed by a golden age of pilgrimages, lasting almost two centuries.

Canterbury was already the destination of pilgrimages to the tombs of St Dunstan and other early archbishops. The Pilgrims' Way, passing through Chevening, Otford and Kemsing, was supposedly used by all the travellers, but Watling Street was a far more logical route for pilgrims from London and the north. Those travelling from Winchester and the west could have had the option of going by way of the new market settlement at Brasted, and past the Hospital of St John the Baptist at Greatness with its own sacred springs and hostel accommodation. The growth of Seal and its eclipsing of its mother settlement at Kemsing appears to be due to its position on a preferred route, which swung to the north east of Seal church, by way of Styant's Bottom and over the centre of Oldbury hillfort. The likeliest explanation was that both routes were used at various times, depending on the state of the road and local flooding. Otford and Kemsing would have been important detours allowing pilgrims to visit St Bartholomew's shrine at the parish church

at Otford, St Edith's chapel in Kemsing churchyard or the holy well in the village centre. Lambarde, writing in 1570, cynically described the fertility cult at Otford church, where suppliants would offer a cock for a male child and a hen for a female.

St John the Baptist's Hospital at Greatness, though first mentioned in 1288, is thought to have been associated with the Saxon chapel of Greatness. Otford Manor House had a large almonry for poor travellers and pilgrims, and the Hospital at Greatness may have begun as a leper hospital. Naturally lepers were housed a good distance away from the manor house, but the hospital's location may also have been connected with the healing powers of the spring.

The Hospital probably also took in travellers, as well as housing the elderly, the sick and the mentally ill. Its likeliest location was just north west of the present Bat and Ball crossroads – until the 19th century a staggered junction since crossroads were regarded with superstition. An

30   The upper High Street of Sevenoaks around 1880 looks virtually unchanged today. This flat lens-shaped area just to the south of the church may be the site of the earliest market in Sevenoaks. At the south end, the lodge of Park Grange blocks the line of the old Tonbridge Road.

existing spring to the south of this junction might be an alternative location, since it is associated with a 19th-century tradition of a holy well to our Lady of Greatness. The hospital had a stone chapel and agricultural buildings associated with the adjacent endowed lands which kept the hospital self-sufficient. In addition there would have been a refectory and a kitchen, and possibly separate houses for the warden and the chaplain.

There were other hospitals and almshouses in Sevenoaks, Shoreham and Lullingstone. Lullingstone's hospital was founded around 1508, and was probably quite small, with no resident master or chaplain. The Shoreham almshouses were founded in 1473 by John Roos for three poor parishioners, preferably widows, who would receive 7d. weekly. The building, in Filston Lane near the junction with Church Road, has Tudor brickwork with tiny stone-headed windows, and might just date from the 1470s.

The almshouses in Sevenoaks were endowed under William Sevenoke's will (he died in 1432),

to keep 20 poor men and women in 'mansion houses'. The same will endowed 'a Grammar School within some convenient House within the said town' for the instruction of poor boys. William himself is said to have been found abandoned in the hollow of a tree by Sir William Rumpsted (or Rumshed) around 1373, who named him and brought him up. Among the many legends associated with his life is one in which he accompanies King Henry V to France, fights at Agincourt and bests the French Dauphin in single combat. He is known to have been an apprentice and then a grocer in the City of London, and in 1418-9 became the Mayor of London, and a close associate of the legendary Richard Whityngton. His coat of arms is the well-known arrangement of seven gold acorns on an azure background, now known as the 'Founder's Arms' of Sevenoaks School.

William Sevenoke's will, unusually, stipulates that the schoolmaster should not be a priest. Most scholars were destined for the priesthood, and he

31 The *Chequers Inn*, seen around 1890 with some of its regulars, profited from its central position in the post-medieval market. The building is said to be a 16th-century rebuild of an earlier inn on the site. Its double-gabled facade has similarities with *Bligh's Hotel*, and both sets of gables may be Victorian additions.

32 L.G. Robinson's 1925 sketch of part of the Shambles (looking east from London Road) is unrecognisable today and shows many since demolished buildings. A very great loss is the building resembling a hall house, with the roof of its recessed hall section carried on brackets.

may have had in mind the broader tuition, suitable for commerce or court, that he may have had himself, or regretted having missed. The actual date of the founding of the school may have been earlier than 1432, possibly in 1418, in a house that Sevenoke owned in the town. There would not be another school in Holmesdale for a century, until one was established during the short life of Otford Palace. It was one of the earliest grammar schools in the country: only Oswestry (1408), Middleton, Lancashire (1412) and Durham (1414) were older.

The growth of the settlement and church at Sevenoaks soon outstripped that of its Darent Valley parents. This was partly due to the success of the nearby submanors at Kippington, Blackhall, Brittains and Knole, whose names are all first recorded in the medieval period, while the original manor of Otford was hemmed in between the steep hillside, the river marshes and the archbishop's deer parks. But it was the thriving market that was the key, a market all the more successful for not being directly under the archbishop's eye, as at Maidstone.

The medieval market in Sevenoaks covered a triangular area from the junction of the Otford and London roads as far north as Bank Street. It seems that the market was the first feature to

appear and required no replanning of an older settlement. Its sloping site, however, has tempted some to look to the flatter open area south of the church as the original site.

The submanor of Blackhall owned six cottages here, lost in the 17th century when the Tonbridge road was diverted from its straight path past the front of Park Grange. The cottages may have had some original market function, perhaps for storage, if they were not actually market stalls. The road to Chiddingstone, now called Oak Lane, drops steeply away from the lens-shaped open area, and the orientation of the Old Post Office, which dates from between 1470 and 1530, suggests a yet wider open space originally. Of the two possible market spaces, one is triangular and one is lens shaped, a pattern found throughout the markets of the South East, Brasted and Westerham for example having both shapes.

Churchyards may have been much more open in early times and are also possible early market areas. The earliest known grave markers are the flat stone coffin slabs, often marked with a cross, that survive at Eynsford church, now relocated to the porch, and at Chevening and Kemsing in their chancels. Markets are known to have been held in early churchyards since Saxon times, judging by the many royal orders against them, though none are known in the Holmesdale valley.

A medieval market cross is known to have existed in Sevenoaks since 1417, and it may have

33 Miss J. Hensman's 1930 sketch of a former market building in the Shambles behind Lloyds Bank records that 'while being demolished this house fell down'. Post-medieval windows cutting across the original framing were probably responsible for the structural weakness. The separation of the building on both sides indicates original alleys.

34 101 High Street (now Millest & Partners) seen in the 1920s, when it was a butcher's shop, a functional link with the Shambles just behind. 8 Dorset Street, next door, has had a facing of timber boarding scored to look like ashlar stone, a regular detail seen in the town.

stood in much the same location as the surviving 19th-century market hall. There was an earlier market house in this position in the 16th century, which was called 'the market cross' in 1682, probably long after the original stone or timber cross had been removed. The market cross was believed to extend a divine protection to bargains struck under it and is likely to have been the earliest feature of the market place, indicating where markets could be held, and perhaps even pre-dating them as a wayside shrine. An alternative possible market cross location might have been near the present *Chequers Inn*, whose name may refer to the chequered cloth on the table where market dues were paid, the same name element found in 'exchequer'. The present inn, said to be Tudor and on the site of an earlier inn, faces onto a surviving small triangular open area which was once called the Butter Market. Another triangular open area is just to the north, at the entrance to the former Lock's Yard. This space may have had some original market function or

may have been where the main track to Knole, via Webbs Alley, originally branched off.

Many early markets have similar triangular open spaces, such as at Brasted and Westerham where the original frontage lines have gradually been set back. Often there was some replanning and rebuilding on the orders of the Lord of the Manor, as with the building of the south side of Dorset Street around 1600. Here substantial cellars for storage were provided which must have made the new buildings very valuable. Stalls built in the market area were laid out in a grid with alleys between them. Some stalls were fairly small, and a rent record of 1492 mentions a parcel of land in the market 'in length seven feet and in breadth two feet' rented by one John Wybourne for one halfpenny; but over time these tiny pieces were combined into larger holdings.

The oldest surviving building in the town (now Calamus) may have been built as a two-storey unheated shop with its first floor open to its crown-post roof. It has been approximately dated to between 1450 and 1530, and was originally detached, with a jettied front onto the Shambles. Other survivals from this period include nos. 99 (*c.*1575-1600) and 101 (*c.*1600) High Street on the junction with Dorset Street. These buildings were also originally detached and surrounded by passageways on all sides, some of which can still be identified today. A major passageway existed running north-south in 1417 and this survives today as the Shambles. Here meat and fish would have been sold, wisely kept apart from other foods to localise unpleasant smells and refuse. Throughout the market, craftsmen would have carried out their trades in their stalls and shops. The medieval house beside Penshurst church lychgate has an early shop window, now filled in, recognisable by its arched head, and may originally have had a timber shutter which doubled as a trading counter. Craft surnames meanwhile became common in medieval deeds.

Sevenoaks's market house was by the mid-16th century an octagonal oak-framed building on posts, and may have replaced an earlier, similar building. It would have functioned in much the same way as Otford's Court Hall, arbitrating disputes and dispensing justice for the market place originally, and then later taking over the manorial courts. It even housed irregular sessions of the Assizes, particularly in the reign of Queen Elizabeth I. These include by tradition the trial of

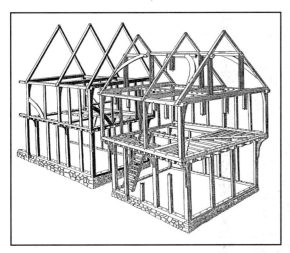

35 Anthony Stoyel's reconstruction of 99 (left) and 101 (right) High Street, Sevenoaks shows the principal framing timbers and conjectural doorways, the latter based on steps in the ragstone base. The alley way separation and jetties are visible, as is the attic floor of no.101.

Henry Isley, Lord of the Manor of Sundridge and a leading member of Thomas Wyatt's failed rebellion against Queen Mary in 1554, who was then executed at Gallows Common, to the west of St John's Hill.

This unusual market building somewhat resembled Maidstone's former Butter Market, perhaps because both markets were owned by the archbishop. The ground floor was originally open with only a stair to the upper level and was traditionally where corn was sold, a link retained when it later became a Corn Exchange. The openings between its eight pillars had flat pointed timber arches and 'Curious lattice work was picturesquely introduced, and the upper story [*sic*] was surmounted by a tiled cone, terminating in a ball, oddly cut, somewhat like the finials on grave rails' (Jane Edwards's description). There was no room for the usual lock-up here, and so the town jail was at nos. 14-18 London Road, most likely in one of the timber-framed ground-floor rooms rather than the more dramatic cellars.

While the market is pre-Conquest in origin and thus predates market charters, it first appears in historical records in the 1280s. One record of 1292 records the grant by Roger de Sevenakes to Robert de la Cnolle (Knole) of shops and plots of ground in the market place. These men were presumably transferring tenancies that they held of the archbishop, the Lord of the Manor.

In the early medieval period, markets proliferated, with beneficial effects on their dependent towns and hinterland. Their importance was reinforced by the strict controls on all transactions, including the straightforward exchange of goods, restricting these to the market place and market day, with severe penalties for transgressors. Dues were levied on the market sellers as a form of taxation; the proceeds going to the lord of the manor, the Crown having claimed its share by the original grant of a royal charter for a weekly market, usually at some expense. A weekly market grant specified both the day of the market and also an annual fair of several days' duration around a saint's day, normally the same as the town's parish church dedication. Sevenoaks's market day appears always to have been on Saturday.

Kemsing was granted a Wednesday market in 1233 during the reign of Henry III. His sister Princess Eleanor owned the manor of Seal and

Kemsing where she retired at the age of 16 (after three years of marriage) on the death of her husband, the Earl of Pembroke. In the same year Henry gave her 20 oaks from his Tonbridge estate to rebuild her manor house after a fire, indicating that the market grant was a revenue-generating gift to help finance the rebuilding. This may have stood near Penfield, to the north of Seal Church, and the annual three-day fair around St Edith's day, 16 September, was to be held nearby. In 1238, Eleanor married Simon de Montfort, who in 1264 defeated King Henry III at Lewes and called the first parliament to include commoners. A year later she had to escape to France when de Montfort was killed at the battle of Evesham. A second Monday market grant in 1366 by Edward III also gave a three-day fair around the festival of St Peter and St Paul, which is the dedication of the church in Seal, suggesting that both were held in Seal.

Brasted contains a number of medieval houses, including 2-5 Alms Row Cottages (1440-80) by the church, and 17 High Street (1440-90). The market town was founded by the Clare family and is recorded as a medieval borough. It must have been intended to grow but probably failed, like others, because it had started after the early medieval boom.

Westerham's market has had three separate charters, in 1227, 1351 and 1619, though it may have been much older. Charter renewals often suggest a right that was not implemented, or had lapsed, which happened if even a single week

36 Brasted green and parish pump, around 1915. The cottages behind must have been built or rebuilt after the Clare family developed the market there. The dentilated gable of one is a vernacular bow towards classicism.

was missed (a token stall would even be put up on Christmas Day, to forestall this).

Annual fairs were important for bringing visitors from much further afield, who would then stay for the duration of the fair. Tolls would be charged on animals and goods brought in. Sevenoaks had two fairs, one around St Nicholas's day (6 December) and one around St Peter's day (29 June), although by Victorian times these had moved to 10 July and 12 October. Otford's fair was based on St Bartholomew's day (24 August), Brasted's on the Thursday in Rogation Week, and Westerham's on the Nativity of Our Lady (8 September). Kemsing and Westerham would later have designated sites, at Fairfield Close in Kemsing, and at the west end of Westerham, opposite the former Black Eagle brewery. Fairs were generally suppressed during the Commonwealth, breaking their historical momentum, and may account for the date changes in Sevenoaks.

The economic boom in the early medieval period was marked by the enlargement of all the churches in Holmesdale. Rituals became more elaborate: at Kemsing a rood screen was erected to heighten the mystery of the chancel. Above it was a statue to St Mary the Virgin, and elsewhere in the church were statues to the Saints Christopher, Margaret and Catherine. A porch was added in about 1341 for marriages, which were held in the open at the church door to be witnessed by all.

St Nicholas' Church at Sevenoaks acquired a north aisle quite early, and in the next century transepts were added, and the chancel extended, to give the whole building a cruciform plan. This expansion reflected the early growth of the town, and was not matched by the other churches in the valley below. Burials at St Nicholas have been found dating from the 12th century, including that of a priest wearing gold trimmed vestments, and a family grave outside the original church walls.

The Chantry Chapel to the south east of the church resulted from an endowment in 1257 by an absentee Rector, Henry of Ghent. This also provided for additional priests to serve at the subaltar to the Blessed Virgin within the chapel, and to say masses for the soul of the Rector's parents and benefactors. The late 17th-century

37 Westerham Green after 1911, with the spire of St Mary's Church breaking the roofline.

house adjoining the churchyard on the south side is called The Chantry and includes a 1686 datestone on its garden wall. It marks the site of either the earlier medieval residence of the chantry priests or the lands that supported them and is said to incorporate part of the Tudor house built after the chantry was suppressed.

Also in the 13th century a tower was built at the north-west corner of the church which, judging from the bell casting pit stained with red dye nearby, was intended to carry bells. The south aisle was added in the same period, and the nave arcade of columns created to give a very large open area. The north aisle was enlarged during the following century, but by 1404 buttresses were being built to shore up the chancel after the Rector had been ordered to make repairs.

The economic boom had begun to falter in the early 14th century. Crops failed, there were long periods of famine, and tremendous storms swept away whole communities along the south-

east coast, reducing the resistance of the population in the decades preceding the Black Death of 1348-9. The Black Death, or bubonic plague, was transmitted by the flea of the black rat, a mammal which lived in close proximity to man. These rats thrived in the insanitary conditions, some even infesting the thatched roofs of houses, and falling, in their own plague death agonies, onto the families sleeping below. The effect of the two plague summers on the people of Sevenoaks and Holmesdale is not directly known. King Edward III celebrated Christmas at Otford Manor in great style in 1348, which is possibly a sign of a healthy neighbourhood. But then winter was a period of respite in the plague, which would return with a vengeance in spring.

There is no record of a parish priest in Shoreham for a 20-year period around this time, and one suspects that he was another Black Death casualty. The churches at Woodlands and Maplescombe, both in the downland area to the north of Kemsing, failed at this time. Woodlands was a particularly small hill-top parish, and its late origins show up in its more English sounding wood-related name (the parallels and contrasts with Sevenoaks are interesting). A third of the national population may have died in the plague and, while there would have been some extreme local fluctuations, failed churches are more likely due to the abandonment of marginal land cultivated in the boom period, than the result of an entire community dying out.

After 1349, labour for the manors was scarce, and attempts to insist on pre-Black Death obligations and wages were ultimately doomed. The Peasants Revolt of 1381 was a stage in this process, a primarily Kentish revolt against high taxation. Archbishop Simon Sudbury, as Richard II's Lord Chancellor, was the main focus of hatred, which culminated in his execution at the Tower of London, where ironically he had taken refuge. His houses in Kent came under attack too, and the records of great expense on stone and timber at Otford Manor in the years immediately after 1381 indicate that it must have been considerably damaged. Great numbers of documents, particularly tax records, were selectively destroyed in the process, much to the chagrin of later historians.

The pastoral economy of Holmesdale meant that manorial obligations were less heavy than elsewhere and perhaps as a result endured longer: the manors of Greatness, Bradbourne, Brittains and Rumsted were still paying rents to Otford in the 16th century, well after Sevenoaks had become independent and with its own submanors, including Knole and Wickhurst.

One consequence of the depopulation caused by the Black Death was the number of new deer parks created on emptied estates, particularly on the poorer soil where there was already unprofitable woodland, such as at Penshurst. Many have not survived except as place names: Park Farm on the north side of Otford was once within Otford Manor's Great New Park, while the older Little Park was to the south of the village extending up to the river Darent. Seal's Park Lane records a 160-acre lost park between Kemsing and Seal, and Morants Court's park also has almost totally been lost. There were deer parks before the Conquest, but most date from the 12th century, when the more easily contained fallow deer

were introduced from the continent. Emparkment required a royal licence, following which parks would be enclosed all round by fences, hedges or ditches, which can sometimes be traced today. Knole alone remains a deer park, having grown considerably in size in the post-medieval period.

The creation of the medieval deer parks may have caused as much disruption as the later landscape parks did. The two manors of Lullingstone Rosse and Lullingstone Payfrere or Peyforer were combined in 1280 and a deer park was created, causing the abandonment of the latter. Its church, St John the Baptist, which was built upon the Roman temple foundations, was also abandoned, and the associated hamlet and Domesday mill removed. The park survived until the last war and today is, in part, a golf course.

Cade's rebellion in 1450 was another primarily Kentish revolt. Reverses in the wars with France were popularly considered to be the fault of William de la Pole, Duke of Suffolk, and James Fiennes, Lord Saye and Sele. Suffolk, banished to France, was intercepted and beheaded on the beach at Dover by political rivals. Fiennes, who was at the time the Lord Lieutenant of Kent, unfairly and somewhat rashly threatened to punish the whole county for this, prompting the rising.

Fiennes was the owner of Knole, an estate which had been carefully assembled by several families over the previous two centuries. He was an able extortioner at a time when fortune seemed to smile on such practices. On one occasion he, with his wife and an associate named Slegge, forcibly persuaded a landowner at Wrotham to

38 *Bligh's Hotel*, once called Bethlehem Farm, seen around 1903. The entrance to its meadow, the future car park, is roughly fenced off.

give him 100 acres of land in Seal. Fiennes then compounded his villainy by extorting double rents from his new tenants in Seal and Kemsing.

Cade's followers met on the heath at Blackheath, but then faded into the Kentish night when a royal army approached. A smaller royal force was sent down under Sir Humphrey Stafford to the 'wood countrie neere unto Sennocke', where it was ambushed and routed at Solefields. Stafford, his brother and 24 others in the King's force were killed, the last one despatched in the doorway of an inn on the site of the present *Dorset Arms*. While this was no great military action, its significance was tremendous. James Fiennes was executed, and it was only the concern of the citizens of London for their property that made them fight back and drive out the rebels. Church leaders acting as mediators brought an end to the revolt and the numerous pardons give an indication of local involvement. These name men, including some from prominent families, from Chevening, Brasted, Sundridge and Westerham, though the people of Sevenoaks seem to have been less involved.

Cade himself was captured after a struggle in a garden in Heathfield and mercifully died of his wounds on his return to London. There were further small risings in Westerham (1453) and Farningham (1454), and a commission investigated some of the alleged abuses of power over the next few years. In the case of William Isle, one of Fiennes's followers and a 'gentleman' of Sundridge, it found him not guilty of various crimes including thefts of animals. Once again Kent had been at the centre of radical protest, typical of the free-thinking communities of the Weald, where the relative isolation from their parent manors to the north had ensured the early development of freer forms of tenure.

The Norfolk family of Bullen or Boleyn had prospered through trade and political power in the City, and bought Hever Castle, another of the late James Fiennes's possessions, in 1462. They also bought the manor house called Burghest Court in Chiddingstone (now the village shop) in 1517. Meanwhile a Chiddingstone yeoman family, the Streatfeilds, were becoming ironmasters in the Wealden iron industry and would later build the 17th-century core of what would become Chiddingstone Castle.

39 A *c.*1800 engraving of the cottage which stood on the site of the Vine Baptist church. The tight proximity to its neighbours may indicate an original hall house with crosswings, perhaps part of the farm that once tended the Archbishop's vines. Another view of the same cottage is in T.G. Jackson's *Recollections*.

Penshurst also prospered as the new county seat of the four times Mayor of London, Sir John de Pulteney, when the earliest parts of Penshurst Place were built for him in the 1330s. The scale of his stone hall house was a reflection more of his great wealth than the economic value of the estate, though he may have been attracted by the deer park. Despite being given a licence to crenellate his house, he did not fortify it, a degree of confidence not apparently shown by the builders of the earliest surviving parts of Ightham Mote, built at around the same period (although the moat may not be contemporary).

Moats, however, may not have been constructed solely for defence. They went through a cycle of being fashionable and, when well-stocked with fish, they were very useful on religious fast days. In certain cases they may have been created to help drainage in damp sites, though in others the site may have been chosen to allow a moat to be built more easily, as perhaps at Hever. The use of puddled clay as a lining material also allowed moats in less obvious sites. Rumsted Manor, near Underriver, in one of its incarnations, occupied a spring-fed moated site on the lower slopes of the Greensand Ridge. The Otford Archaeological Society have dated occupation to shortly after 1280. Henden Manor, south of Ide Hill, also has a moat in a similar hillside location. In the Darent valley, Filston Hall, south of Shoreham, retains a moat whose scale suggests that defence against a local rabble rather than a determined force was intended. Lullingstone Castle's moat, filled in in the 18th century, originally occupied the open area between the 15th-century gatehouse and the present house.

Many other medieval moated sites have been lost, including that of the original manor of Bradbourne for, while moats were highly fashionable in the 12th and 13th centuries, they would later seem outdated and unhealthy. When Otford Palace was built in the early 16th century, it was unusual in retaining its original odd-shaped medieval moated site and cramming its new buildings onto it, a great contrast with the symmetry of its outer court whose remains we see today.

Other sites, particularly on the rising Chartland slopes, appear never to have had moats. Knole is first recorded in 1281 as a personal name, de Knolle, in a land transfer. Its oldest buildings are

on the north side of the present house, a side described by Vita Sackville-West as looking like 'a medieval village' and indeed some of the ragstone walling here may be 13th-century. There is little trace of the medieval origins of other manors which have survived, such as Brittains, Blackhall, Pemley Court (later called Bradbourne), Kippington, Brook Place (later Montreal), Rumstead, and Stiddolphs (later Wildernesse).

All of these early manors were probably timber-framed hall houses. The typical hall house comprised a central hall open to the roof, with single or, more frequently, double storey accommodation to each side. One side contained the private family accommodation, comprising a large upper chamber called the 'solar' above the ground floor 'parlour', from the French verb *parler*. At the opposite end were the service rooms – the kitchen, pantry (bread and dry goods store), the

40 Chiddingstone's two manor houses display their wealth as though in rivalry, creating some of the finest medieval detailing in the south east.

41 Riverhead's Flemish House was an exceptional building and might indeed have had Flemish origins. The massive simple chimney-stack suggests a semi-industrial use, though probably not as the tanyard it became. Patches of missing plaster in this *c*.1900 photograph suggest that poor maintenance was a factor in its loss.

buttery and storage rooms. In the hall the smoke from the fire rose to escape through louvres or by seepage through the roof thatch. Sundridge Old Hall (built *c*.1458) retains its central circular hearth which was originally surrounded by an earth floor. Halls which have been later floored in at first-floor level, can normally be identified by the soot blackening of the roof timbers.

The owners would dine, often on a raised platform, at the private end of the hall. The rectory in Westerham had a timber canopy here where the master sat with his back against the wall looking towards the often highly decorated partition wall fronting the service rooms. This was a pattern repeated in both large and small buildings: Penshurst Place's 14th-century Great Hall (19m. long by 12m. wide), and Archbishop Bourchier's Great Hall at Knole, built about 1460 to replace an earlier hall (which was shortened to become the new kitchen), both had decorated service-end screens.

Houses could be extended by adding cross-wings at right angles, and thus Well Cottage in

42 The *Amherst Arms* (now the *Harvester*) around 1880 has jettying at two levels, often an indicator of a floored-in former hall, but perhaps here was due to the sloping site. The brick building downslope, probably stables, has now become part of the car park.

43 Sundridge's Old Hall seen around 1910. Its forward lean led to major rebuilding works in 1923 which revealed the grooves of storm shutters for the mullion windows which were closed by pegs, a squint to allow approaching visitors to be seen, and external wooden steps to the upper floor probably covered by a lean-to roof.

Sundridge is older than its crosswing, now called Chapman's Farm. Holly Place in Shoreham has an older crosswing, because the original hall burned down and had to be rebuilt in chestnut, a good match visually for oak though not as durable, around 1600.

The upper floors of medieval houses often jetty out, as in the classic Wealden recessed-front house, seen at Sundridge Old Hall, and in several local villages. This was more likely for sound structural reasons, or even for the sake of appearance, rather than to gain extra space on restricted sites, for typically these were isolated farmhouses standing away from village centres. Jettying is structurally economical as it allows the same sized timber to span further than it would otherwise, given that the maximum width of hall houses was governed by the greatest length of oak rafters that could be obtained. A great deal of wealth was tied up in a house, and for a house to be well-built enough to have survived to this day, a minimum holding of approximately 50 acres, excluding woodland, would have been necessary.

The hall house appeared quite suddenly at the beginning of the 14th century, in a paradigm shift, mistakenly called the First Great Rebuilding. Of domestic architecture before that period virtually nothing remains, the timber structures being presumably so technically or stylistically inferior that they were either not considered worth adapting or just fell down. Within a generation a mature technology of oak framing developed, which then changed very little over the next few centuries.

IV

New People and New Ideas

Tudor and Stuart Sevenoaks

Holmesdale was much less affected by the end of the Wars of the Roses and coming of the Tudors than it had been by Cade's rebellion in 1450. But calm had returned by 1456, when the Archbishop of Canterbury, Thomas Bourchier, bought the estate called Knole, near to his manor in Otford, for a trifling £266 13s. 4d. Over the next 30 years he transformed the small stone manor house into something decidedly more palatial. He created a timber-framed court with a surviving stone gatehouse (later completely faced with stone and renamed the Stone Court). His new west front was later encapsulated by a yet larger court, built by either Henry VIII or Bourchier's immediate successors, called the Green Court. Bourchier's gatehouse, though much altered, looks formidable, and includes machicolations (slots for pouring

44   Knole House around 1860.

boiling oil onto attackers) which, though never intended for use, nevertheless conveyed an impression of strength and longevity, strangely at odds with the decorative oriel window below.

Bourchier clearly loved Knole, and he was the first of the archbishops to take more than a financial interest in Sevenoaks. Webbs Alley, the steep and most direct route to his new house, would have been used more frequently than hitherto, and a man-made pond on the slopes below Knole, complete with a ramp into the water, may have been used at this time to refresh horses on the journey to the house and to swell up the timber wagon wheels in dry weather to secure them in their iron rims.

Archbishop Warham restored the influence of Otford by building his new palace there in 1514, demolishing almost all of the old manor house in the process. All that can be seen today of the archbishop's new palace are the ruins of the north-west end of the courtyard north wall. These were built in brick, a material which, until the new Lullingstone gatehouse was built in 1497,

had not been seen locally since Roman times. Both Lullingstone and Otford show a mature craft, probably imported from the Continent, and Lullingstone even has brick machicolations. However, the large area between the gatehouse and the earlier medieval house at Lullingstone then contained an inner gatehouse and moat (removed in the 18th century), as well as the tiny Norman church. At Otford, however, the large, almost square outer court was specifically provided and enclosed for spectacular entertainment. Two-storey galleries ran around three sides of the court, the upper level being timber-framed and open and the lower level cloistered, giving an almost Mediterranean appearance. Behind the galleries were lodging rooms which looked out onto pleasure gardens, providing extra accommodation in addition to a formal court. The symmetry of the courtyard suggests early Renaissance planning, but the irregular heptagonal (seven-sided) walls of the corner towers and the peculiar plan of the house itself, squeezed onto the medieval moated site, belong to an earlier period. Here were the

45 The remains of Archbishop Warham's palace at Otford, with the church in the background. The ivy covered tower was at the north-west corner of a huge courtyard, and the thatched single-storey range was once part of the two-storey north end of this.

Archbishop's hall, chapel, state rooms and other accommodation, of which only a few low level sections of perimeter walling survive now in the front garden walls of Bubblestone Road.

It was probably Warham who rebuilt his reeve's house at the important road junction in Sevenoaks (now Outrams, 63-65 High Street). A fireplace inside has the arms of Warham (1502-32) and Archbishop Chichele (1414-43) in its spandrels. Warham seems partially or wholly to have rebuilt an earlier building by Chichele on the site, and given his reassertion of the importance of Otford, it suggests that he wanted to keep an eye on a useful and perhaps sometimes unruly asset.

The Tudor period of stability allowed the power of central government to grow and consolidate. The considerable resources of the Church were appropriated to finance much social change and to reward the Tudor 'new men', many of whom either came from Kent or had settled in the county. Among these was Thomas Cromwell who leased Filston Manor near Shoreham in 1529, although there is no evidence that he stayed there.

The dissolution of religious houses affected Sevenoaks little, since both St John's Hospital at Bat and Ball and the Chantry at St Nicholas had already ceased to have an active life, and their lands were painlessly absorbed by the Crown. The lands of the Hospital were taken up in the King's deer park and, while the chapel was still in existence in 1607, it had gone by the mid-19th century, some of its stones being used to build Brook Place in Riverhead.

Royal attention now became closely focused on Otford and Knole, in both of which properties Henry VIII had stayed. Archbishop Cranmer inevitably had to accede to Henry's sly request to be given Knole as well as Otford Palace, for the Palace 'standeth low, and is rheumatick, like unto Croydon, where I could never be without sickness. And as for Knole, it standeth on a sound, perfect, and wholesome ground, and if I should make my abode here, as I surely mind to do now and then, I will live at Knole and most of my house shall live at Otford'. Henry later added the submanors of Rumstead and Deanhill (thought to be the site of Sevenoaks School's Manor House) by irresistible offers of land exchanges. The King's interest in Knole is demonstrated by the amount of work carried out for him there in the 1540s, including the new west front, the Green Court and the stocking of the deer park which Cranmer had been too poor to do.

Henry had some repairs made to Otford Palace, but all work ceased with his death and its fate was sealed. Queen Elizabeth's view was that 'sooner shall the house fall and the deer perish than so much money be disbursed' for repairs, and eventually Sir Robert Sidney bought the palace and park in 1601, aiming to build a new house there. This would have been more accessible in winter than his existing seat at Penshurst Place, but his own financial difficulties soon ruled this out. Over the next few centuries the ruins must have been a gaunt reminder of Otford's fall from grace, as well as being a useful source of building stone, some of which may have ended up in Knole's Bird House.

It was during this period that William Lambarde made his *Perambulation* through Kent, which was published in 1570. He noted that many deer parks had been disparked, including one at Otford and those at Panthurst (Sevenoaks Weald), Brasted, Henden (near Ide Hill), and Hever, and that only Otford's Great Park, Knole and Penshurst were still in use. He was particularly exercised by the pre-Reformation religious cults of Kemsing and Otford, and Sevenoaks itself was dismissed with 'and yet finde I not in all historie, any memorable thing concerning it', save for the founding of the school and the battle of Solefields.

The early years of the 16th century had seen some major works to churches in Holmesdale, the first for almost 200 years. New towers or spires were added to the churches at Seal, Chevening and Kemsing. Some work from this period has Catherine of Aragon's pomegranate emblem, as at Otford Church, and may possibly have been connected with royal visits en route to the Field of the Cloth of Gold in 1520. Work stopped again with the more radical Protestant reforms under Edward VI.

The complex nature of the times, where radical and conservative factions at court in turn held sway, can be seen by the martyrdom of John Frith in 1534. Frith had been born in Westerham, where his father kept the *George* inn by the church gateway. The family then moved to another inn in Sevenoaks's upper High Street opposite the present-day vicarage. Frith became a student at William Sevenoke's free school and later went to Eton and Cambridge. He helped Tindale to translate the New Testament into English, but his other activities and writings were pronounced heresy and he bravely went to the stake at Smithfield aged thirty-one.

William Sevenoke's school was granted a new constitution in 1560 by Queen Elizabeth I after her visit to Ralph Bosville at Bradbourne. One of the Tudor 'New Men', Bosville's interest in the school was recent, since he had only bought Bradbourne from the Crown in 1555, but may be an instance of the philanthropist newcomer that would be more evident in the next few centuries. The school was given a new governing body of two wardens and four assistants, and a new name, the Queen Elizabeth Grammar School. There is no record of any tangible change in the school until 1631, when a new stone building was erected. This is thought to have been very small, about 12.5m. by 5m. overall, with two classrooms below and the master's and usher's chamber above in the dormer-lit roofspace.

While many families thrived during the Tudor period, the poor became poorer, largely because of inflation. The effects can be seen in the decline in the number of manorial tenants at Otford, with those remaining adding to their holdings considerably. Few of the tenant families had been in the area a century before, and many were gentlemen with land holdings elsewhere, suggesting a greater geographic mobility than one might expect. The Polhills of Otford, for instance, rose from yeomen to the status of gentlemen in the late 16th century, and almost quadrupled their holdings to 820 acres in 30 years. The plight of the poor was emphasised by the whipping of the unemployed, and the branding of vagrants on the shoulder, while bad weather in the 1590s made things even worse for the landless labourers and those with barely sustainable smallholdings. This growing problem was recognised in the Poor Laws of 1599 and 1601, which made each parish responsible for its poor.

The demise of the old manor and the hundred courts had left a vacancy that was now filled by the parish vestry. The Parish Vestry of Sevenoaks met in a small room over the south porch of St Nicholas Church, and consisted of the vicar, his churchwardens and about ten other appointed officials, including the surveyors of highways, the overseer of the poor, constables and the parish clerk. These officials were overseen by the Justices of the Peace, typically knights or gentlemen from the most important local families who were taking over the responsibilities of the sheriff and judges locally. Other vestries often met in local inns: Otford's met in the *Bull* inn and, while in theory they were open to all householders, they tended to be controlled by the major landowners and tenants in a form of enlightened despotism.

The help they provided for the poor included placing orphans in employment and paying for funerals. The sick and mentally ill might also be cared for and the unemployed put to work, but they were keen to pass on their responsibilities to other parishes, and even those paupers who were accepted did not have an easy ride. In 1644 the poor of the parish of Sevenoaks were ordered by the Vestry to wear a brass badge on their right arm and would forfeit a month's pay if ever seen without it. This practice may have lapsed by 1711, when the Vestry issued a similar order.

Poor houses, where provided, were generally on a small scale, Seal's being built in 1632 for a family who were lying in the street. Chiddingstone workhouse at Somerden Green was a purpose-built structure. It carries the date 1601, perhaps referring to the legislation that brought it into being. Its external form is very similar to no.4 High Street in the village, which has a pargeted date of 1697 together with heart motifs, and this is perhaps the building's true age. The workhouse, probably originally called a Poor House, has a central entrance and chimney stack, and then may have been segregated into a male and female end. Other poor houses were in existing accommodation, such as 20-24 High Street, Otford, and houses rented from Shoreham Mill in the late 18th century.

The Sevenoaks town jail was in London Road, in a building that is now used as a furniture store (14-18 London Road). This has cellars which may have been used for holding prisoners, but it is not known whether it was purpose built. This was probably where local rebels were held after Wyatt's rebellion in 1553, before their summary trial in the market house and the subsequent journey to Gallows Common, west of St John's Hill.

46 Knole's grand staircase (*c.*1605) is an early exercise in creating large dramatic stairs.

47 The Retainers' Gallery at Knole House, painted by the author's great-great-grandfather Samuel Rayner in the mid-19th century.

48 The chapel at Knole.

Shoreham had a strongly built detached structure, of unknown date, near to the present school, which was used as a cage for prisoners, and which survived until very recently. Such buildings were primarily to hold prisoners until trial, following which they would either be hanged, punished by whipping or fines, or freed, longer term detention not being an option. Perhaps it was the folk memory of such hard times that led to the very adverse reaction to the gift of an antique whipping post to the village of Otford in the early years of the present century.

★ ★ ★

A new era at Knole began at the beginning of the 17th century with the arrival of Thomas Sackville, shortly to become the 1st Earl of Dorset. The Sackville fortunes were greatly increased by his father, Sir Richard Sackville, who held various lucrative official posts which earned him the dubious nickname of 'Fillsack'. The family were related to the Boleyns through Richard's mother, who was Queen Anne Boleyn's aunt, and they managed to survive Cromwell's purge of the Boleyns to enjoy favour on the accession of Queen Elizabeth. Thomas himself served Queen Elizabeth and King James I, becoming finally Lord High Treasurer of England and a highly respected elder statesman.

He was given Knole in 1566 but, due to complications arising out of earlier grants to royal favourites and subleases, the Lennards of Chevening remained as tenants for almost 40 years. It was they who built the ragstone garden wall and allowed glass making in the park. Sir Thomas only came into full possession in 1603, when he was aged 67, and spent his last five years completing the major works on the house. The curved stone gables of the famous west front of Knole are his, each with the Sackville heraldic leopard on top, obediently turning towards the entrance towers. These gables are Dutch or Flemish in character, probably a legacy from his ambassadorial visits to the Low Countries, and more often seen in East Kent after the great Walloon influx in the late 16th century.

The Green Court's bay windows were part of the growing fashion for bringing more light into buildings. He also built the Stone Court's Doric colonnade, its underground water reservoirs,

49 Bradbourne's chapel, now the Clock House.

and the '1605' dated lead rainwater pipes, all added piecemeal with a collector's eye.

Inside the house, the dark oak screen in the Great Hall, complete with grotesque figures that may be very early representations of Native Americans, is of this period. The Great Staircase beyond, where barely a square centimetre passes without being decorated, is part of the new interest in the dramatic effect of open staircases that develops throughout the Jacobean period. New state rooms were created on the south side of the Stone Court, and include the Ballroom, the Reynolds Room, the Cartoon Gallery and the King's Bedroom. Walls are decorated with oak panelling and ceilings with deeply moulded plasterwork in geometric patterns, and the enormous polished stone and marble fireplaces are focal points in each room. Thomas Sackville's successors, the Earls and Dukes of Dorset, did not greatly alter the building, although several added significantly to the furniture and painting collections and to the parklands, leaving a remarkably unaltered 17th-century house.

The Bosvilles were another new Tudor family, coming to Bradbourne in 1555, and holding it

until 1761. Bradbourne was probably a timber-framed manor house, surrounded by a moat in the earlier days, only being replaced with a stone mansion in 1689. The Bosvilles, the town's second family, found the journey uphill to the church at St Nicholas a great burden 'for almost all the winter and in other rainy and stormy days', and obtained permission in 1614 to build a chapel in their own grounds. Now much altered and more resembling a watchtower, it was used in its time for the baptisms, marriages and funerals of family members and servants. Few private chapels were built so late (although St Clere's, consecrated in 1633, is later); and, while local roads must have been awful in winter, perhaps there was also a desire to emulate the Sackvilles, who had their own private chapel at Knole.

Chevening House and St Clere, near Kemsing, both date from the early 17th century, a period advantageous for building large houses because of low taxes and low poor rates coupled with rising prices. Chevening was built by Lord Dacre, probably just before 1630, and replaced an Elizabethan house, fragments of which survive in the cellars and possibly in the salon or dining room. It is said to have been designed by Inigo Jones, although John Webb has been suggested as an alternative, if the house were actually built nearer the middle of the century. The design is revolutionary, a great contrast to Knole where piecemeal growth resulted in many courtyards surrounded by long two-storey ranges unified by a rhythm of Jacobean gables and stone mullioned windows. Chevening, meanwhile, was a unity, containing all the required accommodation in a single, largely brick-built, classical building. The main floor was raised half a level creating a 'piano nobile', and allowing service rooms to be installed underneath, a pattern that was being repeated 200 years later in the speculative houses of St Johns Road in Sevenoaks.

The internal plan became known as 'double pile': two rows of rooms on the main facades, with a central corridor or other means of access between them. It is a neat and economic form, and its admirers claimed its rooms were neither too hot nor too cold. Lady Dacre's nephew, Roger North, however, was unimpressed, saying that 'all the noises of an house are heard

everywhere', and 'which is worse, all smells that offend, are a nuisance to all the rooms, and there is no retiring from them'. He also did not like the way that ceiling heights were the same in major and minor rooms, and preferred houses which were more spread out. General James Stanhope, who acquired the house in 1717, must have concurred with him, and extended the house to create just such an effect.

St Clere, near Kemsing, also dates from the early 1630s, and its rectangular, brick-built, double-pile arrangement (although without a central corridor) naturally suggests links with Chevening. It is slightly less graceful than Chevening, having almost Tudor octagonal turrets at the corners of the front facade, and a central crest of chimneystacks and is probably the work of a different architect.

In Sevenoaks in 1630, Thomas Farnaby bought Kippington for £2,200, bringing with him his very successful school for the sons of the nobility, which he had run first in Somerset and then in London. His earlier life had been full of adventures in the Caribbean with Drake and Hawkins,

50 St Clere's south elevation shows the off-balancing service wing to the east which must have started the tendency of the house to look towards Kemsing and Holmesdale centuries before it left Ightham parish.

an active role in the War of the Spanish Succession in the Netherlands, and then time as a very poor peripatetic teacher in the West Country. He had had Catholic sympathies as a youth, but he was probably attracted as much by the flamboyance of the Royalist cause. For it he would endure sequestration and a spell in Newgate gaol, while the Civil War divided Holmesdale as it did all England. Local opinions were typically moderate, however, Wealden areas tended to be radical, while the original lands of Holmesdale and the Downs were on the whole more Royalist.

The Polhill family, farmers in Otford, may have had Puritan sympathies since Thomas Polhill married Elizabeth Ireton of Filston, Oliver Cromwell's granddaughter, after the Restoration. Another local family rescued the head of Cromwell, disinterred and detached from his body after 1660, and kept it at Frankfield, Seal Chart, until the early years of the present century.

Edward Sackville, the 4th Earl of Dorset, was very close to the King, and his wife was governess to the King's children. Parliament wisely pre-

empted any hostile moves he might take by sending a force to arrest him in 1642. Knole was seized and later became the site of the provisional Government of Kent by the County Committee. The following year, about 4,000 Royalist supporters assembled on the Vine, but two days of continuous rain dampened their enthusiasm for any action and a Parliamentarian force found only a few hundred left. These were chased towards Tonbridge and dispersed after a short skirmish. In April 1645, the Harts of Lullingstone Castle gathered 800 soldiers to revolt against the County Committee, now based in Aylesford Priory, but again the rising was easily quashed.

Knole escaped sequestration in the aftermath of the Civil War, but the Sackville family were heavily fined. Much worse for the family was the murder of their youngest son after capture at the Battle of Abingdon. Kippington and Sevenoaks Park were sequestrated due to the activities of their owners, Thomas Farnaby and George Lone, who had been prominent leaders of the assembly on the Vine. The Farnabys regained Kippington

51 Park Place in 1818, some decades before the Lambardes would depart and Park Grange would be built on its site. The house was probably put together using pattern books which insisted on at least one Palladian window. The south wing meanwhile seems to have a Kentish mansard roof.

52 The relaxed common settlement of Godden Green in the early 1900s, showing the pond outside the *Buck's Head* public house, and the double-Y road junction with, at the north end, one of the Wildernesse House lodges.

with the Restoration, while George Lone was forced to sell Sevenoaks Park to Thomas Lambard in 1654, thus ending the fortunes of the Lone family locally. Sevenoaks Park, or Park Place (on the site where Park Grange now stands), had come into being after 1500 when 100 acres between Oak Lane and the future Solefields Road and Hopgarden Lane were emparked, probably by John Wildgoose. The Lone family of Rumshed Manor had acquired it in 1559, and Thomas Lambard's renaming the property Brick House suggests that this may have been an early Tudor brick building.

Thomas Lambard also diverted the Tonbridge road, from its straight line from the school past his house to its present position, demolishing in the process several buildings he had acquired. This created a more dignified open space on the east side of his house and more or less by chance has given the town its very dramatic entry from the south.

The post-medieval population growth, a result in part of the relative political stability of the times, led to a renewed pressure on land. Squatter's rights to land could often be obtained by building a dwelling overnight, which may have

happened in 1516 when an illegal squatter cottage was recorded at Godden Green. In 1589 new houses were required to have four acres of land in order to limit subdivision and ensure that householders could sustain themselves and not become paupers. This forced the problem even further to the margins, to the commons and the wastes, because the rising population clearly had to go somewhere.

The plight of the homeless at the time is illustrated in the story of Peter Ware and his young pregnant wife, who were living 'in or under an oak' to the south of Riverhill in the late 16th century. Their situation was desperate, and finally he set up a shelter using four 'scratches', timber poles with the branches still on them, and a roof of thatched straw or grass. Samuel Lone, the owner of Rumshed Manor, took pity on them, allowing them to continue to live on his land. Their shelter survived in some form for a century, occupied in turn by the descendants of the original couple, until the family finally disappeared from the historical record.

New settlements sprang up on the commons, generally at road junctions or around an original farmhouse. Often they were given a 'Green' name, such as Godden Green, Bessels Green and Dunton Green, as they enclosed a green area. Other new settlements included Ide Hill, Sevenoaks Weald, Ivy Hatch and Toys Hill. These 'green' villages were perhaps a reinterpretation of the medieval village, an image which would be further developed in the 19th century at Leigh and Penshurst.

Improve road communications also led to migration to new street villages. At Seal the new turnpike road in 1765 prompted more building along its length, and to a lesser extent between the original core by the church and this new street settlement. Fortunately, the two were only 100m. or so apart, allowing Seal to remain a single village. The new settlement at Dunton Green had already begun in medieval times, drawing occupants from Otford to its core near the junction of the Shoreham valley road and the road to London via Star Hill. By the early 17th century,

two of Otford's four public houses were in Dunton Green, with one, the *Chequers* (now the *Rose and Crown*) apparently being built on the original green. Later growth would be primarily southwards towards the old bridge at Longford, until in the 20th century it would effectively join up with Riverhead.

The hamlet at Norman Street preserved the 'Street' name of its origins (its prefix is thought to mean No Man's Land, or common), though it has since been eclipsed by Ide Hill. Ide Hill's remoteness from its parent village of Sundridge greatly disturbed Bishop Porteus, the Bishop of London, who had a summer residence from 1783 at Bishops Mead in Sundridge. He bought land for the first chapel in Ide Hill, built in 1807, and replaced by the present church in 1860.

Sevenoaks Weald began as a less focused common settlement which had formed around road

53   The Bowyer family pose outside Kemsing's 16th-century Old Vicarage (now Vicarage Cottages) around 1897. The growth of ivy and creepers resulted from Victorian romanticism which studiously ignored building maintenance considerations.

54   The 18th-century Buttery on Westerham Green.

and track intersections. In more recent times, gaps have been infilled to create a nucleated village. Deepden Green, or Dibden, has not fared so well, although being in the Kippington estate it may never have been a 'green' settlement as such. Its failure may be linked with the decline in 'ripier' traffic along the fish road from Rye, while Bessels Green would survive thanks to its position on the Holmesdale valley turnpike road.

Religious and political non-conformism was often associated with the new common settlements and with parish boundaries, which tended to be less obviously visible to magistrates and courts. Protestant refugees had been arriving in England since the 1560s, but they settled primarily in east and mid-Kent, and it was not until the 18th century that Huguenot families like those of Peter Nouaille at Greatness and Reverend Vincent Perronet at Shoreham arrived in Holmesdale.

The new ideas were given impetus by the abuses of the established clergy who were all too often absent from their parishes, taking the tithes and leaving impoverished curates to carry out their duties. John Donne, who became Rector of Sevenoaks in 1616 through the gift of his patron, the 3rd Earl of Dorset, may never have preached at St Nicholas. The curates who carried out ministries on behalf of these absent clerics were

meanwhile supporting families on stipends for single priests, which had been devalued dramatically by a century of inflation.

The Commonwealth brought greater freedom of worship for non-conformists over the next two decades and by 1663 dissenters were meeting monthly at Bradbourne. After the Restoration in 1660, however, came a time of intermittent persecution, and non-conformism submerged once again. Meetings would be held in members' houses in out of the way places, such as John Colgate's house Quarnden in Bessels Green. The Colgate family of artisans and farmers illustrates well the character of these early dissenters, typified by a thirst for education and self-improvement. In the 1790s, one member living in Filston continued the dissenting tradition, fleeing from impending arrest for his republican sympathies to America where his family would later found the huge toothpaste empire.

The 1689 Toleration Act extended freedom of worship to non-conformists, with the exception of Catholics, but it was not until 1716 that the first Baptist chapel was built in Bessels Green. This is a simple building with tall clear windows for the light of reason to flood in, and still has a tranquil air which surprises, given its position by the busy A25.

In Westerham, several small traders obtained a market grant in 1619. They leased a piece of waste ground by the *George* inn from the Lord of the Manor for 21 years and built a market house, complete with lantern and bell, for £120 and 13 shambles for £80. An early 19th-century engraving shows the Buttery, an ungainly and out-of-scale open structure on the village green, which may have been this market house or an 18th-century replacement, and whose removal at the end of the 19th century would not be mourned. It was one of the last market grants in Kent. Improvements in transport, with the 18th-century turnpike roads and later by rail, made larger and more specialised markets more accessible, and Westerham's own cattle market was one of these beneficiaries. The greater freedom which allowed buying and selling outside the market place hastened the decline of generalised local markets.

Responsibility for the condition of roads rested with individual parishes, resulting in greatly varying conditions and no overall concern for the increasing numbers of long distance travellers, for whom there were a number of 'road books' being produced in the 17th century. Lord North's discovery in 1606 of medicinal springs between Tonbridge and Frant, was a driving force for change. The route to the springs, later to become known as Tunbridge Wells, was through Sevenoaks, benefiting local inns and traders. The new bridge built at Longford in Dunton Green in 1636 was a highly welcome improvement for those travelling by coach to take the waters, as Queen Henrietta had done in 1630.

Local wealth and social status can be gauged indirectly through Hearth Tax returns from 1662 onwards. Hearths (fireplaces) and chimney flues were not original features of medieval oak-framed houses. Smoke bays of lath and plaster, built like hoods over open fires to channel the smoke up to vents in the roof, were a terrible fire risk. Traces of one survive in Laundry Cottages (49-51 High Street), Westerham. From the 16th century onwards, however, brick became the ideal material for hearths and chimneys, and by the 17th century more localised production was making it more affordable. At Knole, whose Hearth Tax return showed 85 hearths, the original brick chimneys date from the mid-16th century and consist of six flues clustered together, creating strong

forms which balance well with the house entrance turrets and curved gables.

The tax returns list those paying the tax, rather than the buildings themselves, and this can be deceptive where individuals owned several properties. Gentlemen typically had five or more hearths. George Polhill was clearly Shoreham's first citizen by virtue of his 12 hearths, while his kinsman, David Polhill, had 26 hearths at Chipstead Place, the house he had just bought in 1658. At the other end of the scale, there were 20 dwellings in Shoreham with only one, presumably the all purpose kitchen hearth. These and others receiving poor relief were exempt from paying 2s. per year per fireplace.

The returns also show the decline of Otford, with only 37 of its 53 households paying the tax. Sevenoaks, Seal and Sundridge were the most populated parishes, while Halstead, Kemsing and Leigh were the least populous. Chevening parish (which still included Chipstead) had the greatest poverty, with only half of its 99 households chargeable, and was closely followed by Sevenoaks Weald, both parishes containing a high proportion of squatter settlements, where a broken down hovel was the first step to a new life. Riverhead, with the greatest proportion of chargeable households, must have seemed far more affluent with more new houses than surrounding settlements.

Families averaged four individuals, for this was a time of low population growth and around one in six families had servants, as it was not unusual even for labourers to have servants. The demise of the Great Hall, where servants had slept in medieval times, meant that other forms of accommodation were needed. Many new houses had purpose-built attics, and the Kentish mansard roof was very useful for housing servants (for example, nos. 8 and 40 London Road). Other houses sprouted dormers to light the roof-space, such as the long cat-slide roof near the top of Six Bells Lane. The Queen Anne frontage of Little Underriver (now called Underriver House) was built with a usable attic and dormer windows from the start, and as an unusual refinement gave the dormers glazed side cheeks for greater light. The attic servants' quarters have the wide 300mm. floor boards also found in medieval houses (the family rooms below being floored with narrower,

55 The Georgian affluence of Riverhead had lapsed a little by the time of this photograph of the High Street around 1900, looking south from the Seal Road junction towards the gate to Montreal Park (now the Harvester Car Park). Road widening has since torn out the row of houses on the left, and the *White Hart* public house is now a lay-by to a parade of shops.

more regular boards) and a much smaller second stair down to the kitchen.

The medieval house did not hide away its servants. The first moves in this direction were the corridor galleries which gave greater privacy to rooms, such as the Brown Gallery at Knole (*c.*1460); and it is a fair assumption that some of Knole's reputed 50 or so stairways were added later to separate circulations. The newer houses could go much further. Chevening House and St Clere are both early 17th-century houses, and have basement stories to house kitchens and service rooms, together with attic rooms and second stairs.

Houses were changing. New materials were becoming more widely available, and were now locally produced. Local brickfields made brick a cheaper material and it gained such high status that it came to be used for main facades, relegating stone to the less prominent sides and rear, as at the Queen Anne style Rectory at Penshurst. The Great Fire of London of 1666 and the consequent building legislation in London had little direct effect in Holmesdale, but people were already aware of the risk of fire. Clay roof tiles were a great improvement over thatch and oak

shingles, and the resulting less steep roof pitch can still be seen on the tower of Chiddingstone Church, following a major fire there in the late 1620s. Brick chimneys were one of the first additions to the old oak-framed houses in the Second Great Rebuilding, a term describing the wholesale changes undergone by medieval houses in the 16th and 17th centuries to provide improved comfort, privacy and quality of life.

Tudor chimneys were highly decorated but expressed each flue separately. Later, as at St Clere, the mid-17th-century flues were gathered together to form an ungainly roof crest. With the loss of the open fire, most halls were floored in at first-floor level to give extra space and smaller rooms could now have their own fireplaces, rather than having to cluster around the edge of the central hall. Kitchens, often isolated as separate buildings, could more safely be brought into the house. Ladders to upper rooms were replaced by proper staircases, which became increasingly important as architectural elements in the 17th century. The Great Staircase at Knole was one of the first, although the remarkable oak inlaid spiral stair at Chevening House, built in the 1720s, is probably the most advanced.

Glass remained a considerable expense. Medieval timber mullioned windows were small: literally 'wind holes'. Weatherproofing was commonly by sliding timber shutters, evidence of which has been found at Holly Place, Shoreham, or by other methods such as the rabbit skin coverings claimed by Pitts Cottage, Westerham. Yorkshill Farmhouse, near Ide Hill, has a window with timber tracery of similar design to the stone windows of churches, which has managed to survive through being walled in early in its life.

Major improvements in glass production came about from the 1570s onwards, when French and Dutch glassworkers arrived, possibly as Huguenot refugees. In the 1580s the Knole estate records mention timber harvesting for the glass-making furnaces. These may have been near the entrance of Beechmont Farm, off Gracious Lane; an area called Glashowesland a half century previously. The furnace was worked by four men, one named Brussell, possibly a Fleming. In the following century, with the use of coal as fuel, the cost of glass fell until even the poorest could afford it. Glass use was not diminished by the window taxes levied between 1696 and 1851 which are often credited, usually wrongly, with causing the occasional blind window seen in the area.

Most domestic windows consisted of diamond shaped glass quarries in lead cames in a side hung iron frame, opening outwards. The diamond shape allowed the use of smaller glass pieces around the edge, as well as resisting the tendency of the lead to buckle. Timber sash windows using much larger pieces of glass came to the country from the Netherlands in the late 17th century, and became the standard for the next two centuries. A poor man's version of this was the horizontally sliding window, seen in the Old Post Office opposite Sevenoaks School, and dating from the next century.

As glass became more readily available, the type and style of window changed. Bow and bay windows became fashionable in the 16th and 17th centuries; the stone bays in Knole's Green Court date from the arrival of the Sackvilles in 1605. Palladian or Venetian windows, an arched headed window flanked by two smaller rectangular ones, were perhaps copied by travellers on their Grand Tours of Europe and later inserted into their houses with no particular regard for appropriateness, as at Park Place, Sevenoaks and at Ightham Mote.

In churches, the loss of stained and coloured glass at the hands of Henry VIII, Oliver Cromwell and worst of all, neglect, brought much more light into churches as they were replaced by plain glass windows. This worked well with the new Protestant ethos, allowing congregations to read the tablet boards and banishing the forces of darkness and superstition, at the dawn of the Age of Reason.

V

Georgian Order

Eighteenth-Century Sevenoaks

In 18th-century Sevenoaks and Holmesdale the pattern of major estates and houses changed little. The arrival of new families or new wealth would often prompt a rebuilding, but none of the new houses would rival Knole or Chevening architecturally.

The Polhill family had been tenant farmers in Otford for much of the Middle Ages, until their growing fortune allowed them to buy the Chipstead estate with its Elizabethan house. In 1665 they moved back to Otford, to Broughton Place, and it was a subsequent owner, William Emerton, who built Chipstead Place around 1700. The Polhills must have been impressed, moving back to Chipstead in 1710. They soon replaced its cupola, perhaps following many leaks, and a new hipped roof and portico were added. The house kept them in Chipstead until 1829, but only fragments of it remain today; the later ball-room at the west end, the east-end stable block with its strange rocket-like roof vent, and of course the lodges and estate wall in Chipstead Lane.

Riverhill House was built in the early 18th century for the Children family. The turnpike

56 The south elevation of Chipstead Place seen from near its croquet lawn. The pathway at the right of the picture survives in a number of the gardens of houses now built on its grounds.

57 Chipstead Place's stable building survives in part today but the large, louvred lantern, presumably for ventilation, has gone.

road, built in 1710, now allowed carriages to reach the property, and the Tudor farmhouse built by the Petts was pulled down (although its cellars still exist below the present house). The new house began as a small two-storey Queen Anne building, but another storey and dormers had been added by the time an etching was made in 1730. The dormers have since gone, but the proportions

58   The south elevation of Riverhill House in 1842.

of the house have suffered from the extra height and from the two floors of bathrooms added above the entrance porch in this century.

The Stanhope family came to Chevening House in 1717, paying £28,000 for the house and its 1,400 hectare estate. General James Stanhope had distinguished himself in the War of the Spanish Succession by capturing Port Mahon and the island of Minorca, and later became first Secretary of State, First Lord of the Treasury, Chancellor of the Exchequer, and finally Earl Stanhope in 1718. Together with his wife, Lucy Pitt, he extended the house on both sides with pavilion-like service wings, built the magnificent spiral stair, and cut the 'keyhole' through the woods on the ridge crest. Both James and Lucy died young, and their son Philip did not take over the house till more than a decade later, in 1735. He was a scholar of mathematics and languages, and wisely left the running of the estate to his wife, Grizel.

The Stanhopes deserted Chevening House for ten years between 1764 and 1774 to live in Geneva, for the sake of the health of their only surviving son, who was perhaps asthmatic. The correspondence during this period between Countess Stanhope and her steward John Brampton is fascinating. She questions and instructs him in great detail: concerned about the income of the estate and suspicious that tenants and employees were either not working hard enough or were trying to take liberties. He in return gives her the local news she was missing and tries to soften the impact of her strongly opinionated instructions. He criticises the new balcony in Chevening Church knowing her dislike of it, but also pleads on behalf of the deserving poor. In October 1766, for example, there were a number of cases of ague, or malaria, then very common in the valley basin settlements. She recommends a chamomile and brandy recipe for its relief, while he regales her with choice morsels, such as 'the whole talk in the neighbourhood is of Mr Polhills Marriage to one of his Maids', who, it transpired, was pregnant.

Grizel's son, Charles, survived to become the 3rd Earl in 1786 and, while an accomplished inventor (he built a primitive computer and an iron printing press), he had little idea of building maintenance. He thought that the nearly metre-

59 Chevening Place seen from the north in T.M. Baynes's 1830 drawing, shows the 1st Earl Stanhope's flanking pavilions, and his grandson Charles's top-floor extension, now removed.

Needless to say, this roof also failed, and was entirely removed and restored in the 1970s.

Charles Stanhope also has the distinction of making the only known diversion of the Pilgrims' Way around his estate in 1785 from its original line crossing a few hundred metres north of the church and house. More significant was his closure of the old Rye fish road, although a path survives on a slightly different line running north from the church. By this time the Rye road had not passed through Chipstead or Chevening for over a century, going instead through Sevenoaks and Riverhead and over the new Longford bridge. Chevening became the archetypal estate village, consisting of the big house, the church, and a row of neat retainers' cottages at the end of a cul-de-sac. Of these cottages, nos.6-8 are the oldest, a 17th-century timber-framed house which was refaced with brick in the 19th century. Lennard Lodge (named after the family who bought the earlier house at Chevening in 1551 for £420), opposite the church, was *The Stanhope Arms* public house in the 19th century and later became a post office.

thick walls of the house were letting damp through, and first added a form of render which failed, and next a layer of yellow mathematical tiles. The damage to the original brickwork by the rusting iron nails necessitated its almost complete replacement in the 1970s, when the tiles were taken down. Meanwhile, when the roof leaked, Charles added a patent flat roof and raised the external walls to form a surrounding parapet.

60 Combe Bank's stable block seen in 1917, when the owner, Robert Mond, had converted it into a chemical laboratory.

61 Montreal House at Riverhead in 1819 (drawn by J.P. Neale) shows the projecting pavilion and the rise on which the house was seated.

In return for the closure of these and other paths Stanhope agreed to build the new roads west and east of Chevening crossroads, running up to Sundridge and joining the Star Hill road respectively.

'Citizen Stanhope' was an eccentric liberal, who once forced a vote in the House of Lords against unanimous opposition, for which feat a medal was struck commemorating the 'Minority of One'. His eccentricity was inherited by the daughter from his first marriage to his cousin Lady Hester Pitt, Lady Hester Stanhope, who died in the Lebanon, revered as a queen by her Druze tribesmen followers.

Sundridge's manor had been divided after the decline in the Isley fortunes in the 1550s. Combe

Bank, the northern part of the estate, was bought in 1720 by Colonel John Campbell, later the 4th Duke of Argyle. The original house was replaced in the 1730s by his architect Roger Morris. A contemporary engraving shows a formally awkward two-storey square building with four projecting square corner turrets, almost like a Palladian interpretation of a castle.

His son, Lord Frederick, doubled the size of the property in the 1790s by extending to the north, and commissioned the Adam ceiling which was not in fact installed until the beginning of the 20th century. He also converted the original road north from Sundridge, which ran alongside the east side of the house, into a private drive, recessing it into the ground as a 'ha ha'. Convicts were used to build this and the diverted main road, loaned by a 'neighbour from Penshurst', in much the same way as his father had used the regiment camped at Combe Bank in 1745 to dig a lake for him. Tragedy, however, struck in 1807 when Lord Frederick's wife, Mary, died in a fire which started in the new wing of the house. Their daughter, who had described the house as 'pretty, but cold beyond imagination', sold the house on inheriting it in 1816.

62 Greatness House in the late 18th century with perhaps some of the Filmer family sitting by the lake.

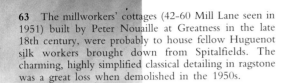

63 The millworkers' cottages (42-60 Mill Lane seen in 1951) built by Peter Nouaille at Greatness in the late 18th century, were probably to house fellow Huguenot silk workers brought down from Spitalfields. The charming, highly simplified classical detailing in ragstone was a great loss when demolished in the 1950s.

64 The south side of Kippington House in the middle part of the 19th century shows the junction of the two-storey original house with the later three-storey rear extension.

The Amherst family came to Brook Place, near Riverhead, in the early 18th century. This was a Tudor house built by the Colepepers, apparently using stones from the old hospital of St John the Baptist at Greatness. Its name suggests that it was close to the string of stream-fed fishponds to the south of the village. Their son Jeffrey became a page in the household of the affable Lionel Sackville, 1st Duke of Dorset, who launched him in an army career which culminated in the North American campaign of the Seven Years War. General James Wolfe of Westerham captured Quebec, while Amherst took his army through the forest wilderness to capture Montreal and secure French Canada in 1760.

On his return to England he built Montreal House on the hilltop above the fishponds, once again reusing stones from the newly demolished Brook Place. He also acquired new land to make a landscaped park which stretched from the back of the present-day Riverhead Harvester to Brittains Farm in Brittains Lane, along Worships Hill to Bessels Green, and along Coldharbour Lane to Salters Heath.

His house faced south, following the new rational understanding of orientation that was replacing the more quasi-mystical ideas of earlier centuries. It was a relatively small house on a natural rise of the ground, built to a Palladian plan and with single-storey pavilions on either side housing the service spaces, kitchens and stables. Kitchens, once detached from the medieval hall house as a fire risk, had been brought into the unified Palladian house, as at St Clere, yet now the extended building complex was returning. The impression of wings embracing the countryside would reappear in later houses such as Wildernesse, Vine Court and Park Place, all of which have small vestigial symmetrical projections at each end of the facade, while outbuildings would be added to Chevening and St Clere on the more formal, front entrance sides.

Greatness House may have been built in the 1760s when the Nouailles started their silk mill nearby, although surviving photographs seem to show an early 19th-century building. On Andrews and Drury's 1769 map it appears as a large building, the size of Bradbourne, with formal gardens to the south and a lake between it and the mills, though this may have been the earlier millowner's house rebuilt by Peter Nouaille and his wife, Elizabeth Delamore of Greatness.

Kippington House was rebuilt in 1780 by Sir Charles Farnaby, retaining only some of the original cellars. He used red brick, now concealed by a coating of stucco, and gave the house its entrance portico. His father Thomas, great grandson of the Thomas Farnaby who had purchased Kippington, had restricted himself to rebuilding Brittains Farm in 1751 (and its oasthouse the

65 The north elevation of Brasted Place around 1922, with the original Adam house on the left, and Waterhouse's French Gothic folly on the right.

66 The back (south) elevation of Brasted Place with Adam's sandstone portico around 1917.

67 The ragstone Bradbourne Hall house had some uncomfortable proportions, the lower, relatively windowless block (housing the Drawing Room) not balancing the taller main building. The surviving lakes are beyond the house.

previous year) presumably on or near the site of the original medieval manor. However in 1796 the Farnabys sold their home to Francis Motley Austen of the Red House in Sevenoaks.

Brasted Place was built for Dr. John Turton in 1785, on the site of the older manor house, called Stockets. Dr. Turton was physician to, among others, the royal family, Garrick, Goldsmith and Horace Walpole, and despite his wealth the new house was very modest, supposedly to deter George III from visiting his wife Mary. The dramatic garden-side portico of the house belies the fact that the rooms, though large, are quite few in number: there are only four family bedrooms. The architect was Robert Adam (who had also worked on nearby Combe Bank and Chevening House), who built it in the golden coloured Tunbridge Wells sandstone. He also built a picturesque bridge (dated 1796) crossing a glen in the grounds and which had been described as being on an ancient trackway. The portico was designed as the focus of a vista between trees on the rising ground to the south, though it is interesting that Adam kept this dramatic feature for the rear of the house. The King cannot have been too displeased, however, as he gave the Turtons an old turret clock from Horse Guards Parade, which still survives on top of the former stable block (now a private house) in The Carriageway nearby.

The Red House in Sevenoaks High Street was built in 1686 for Thomas Couchman, replacing an earlier presumably timber-framed house built by John Gylbert, gentleman. Dr. Thomas Fuller, the pharmacist, bought it in 1688 and in time added the two side wings. Dr. Fuller prided himself on having tested all his preparations on himself, all the more impressive since some remedies included live millipedes and woodlice, spiders' webs, earthworms, powdered bees and dried mouse flesh. In 1743 The Red House was bought by a lawyer, Francis Austen. His great-niece, Jane Austen, stayed a month here in July 1788, aged 12, and it has been suggested that the village of Hunsford in *Pride and Prejudice* was derived from

68 *(right)* Kipp's engraving of the Red House shows a much smaller building than at present, with ornamental and kitchen gardens reaching up to the park pale of Knole.

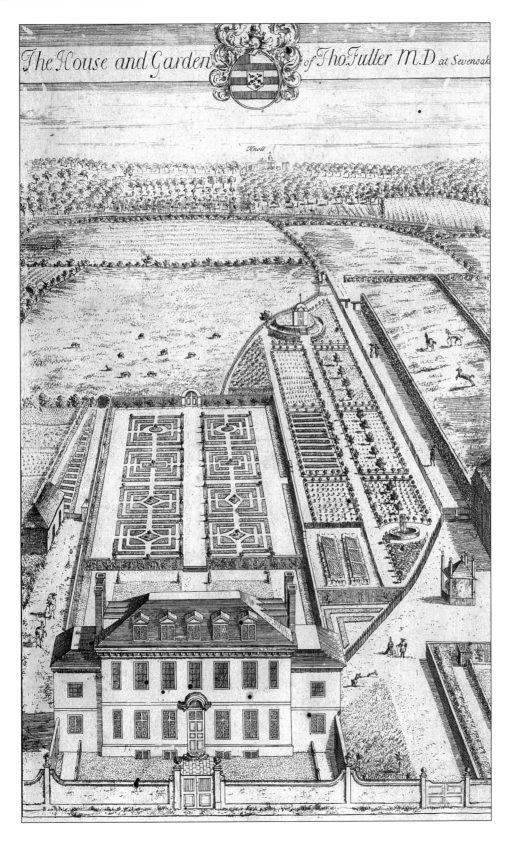

The House and Garden of Tho. Fuller M.D at Sevenoaks

Eynsford, and that 'Rosings Park' was based on Knole or Chevening. Jane, however, does not seem to have been among the family members who carved their initials on the brick wall of the present Christian Science Reading Room to the south of the Red House.

Eight years later the Austens left the Red House for Kippington, and the building became for the next 60 years the 'Sevenoaks Academy' for young gentlemen, founded by the French Revolution refugee, John Baptiste Anquetil. Since 1936 it has been the offices of Knocker and Foskett, solicitors, who moved here from the White House opposite.

The Grammar School and almshouses of 1631 were said to be 'very ruinous and decayed' by 1721, though the cause of this dereliction is unclear. The splendid laziness of Elijah Fenton, master from 1706 to 1710, who, though 'an excellent versifier' according to Dr. Johnson, used to 'lie abed and be fed with a spoon', suggests that simple neglect was a prime factor.

Proposals for rebuilding were made by the Wardens and Assistants who sold land in Billingsgate endowed by William Sevenoke, raising £2,500 and an annual rent of £550. Surviving drawings by Richard Boyle, Lord Burlington, one of the major exponents of Palladianism, show a tall central school building with arcade-fronted almshouses immediately flanking. It seems likely that Boyle took no further interest, however, and

69 Sevenoaks School in 1862, showing the original 1720s buildings before the side wings were raised. The executed design is very different from the surviving Burlington drawing, and seems more a piece of Sevenoaks vernacular. The luxuriant vegetation of the forecourt and the boys' mortar board hats are interesting features.

the design then developed out of a cumulative series of small alterations and adaptations. The major change, setting back the school to create a forecourt, has given a far greater sense of drama and has also allowed the school to grow laterally. The almshouses meanwhile have lost Burlington's arcade and have developed central arched gateways through to backyard areas with rows of neat privy doors. The rebuilding took many years (from 1724 to 1735) and suffered several delays. Frost damage in 1728 was so severe that the half-built structure required demolition, and then a Chancery action for maladministration was brought by Dr. Fuller and parishioners against the warden and the four assistants (Farnaby of Kippington, Lambard of Sevenoaks Park, Bosville of Bradbourne and Petley of Riverhead).

At about this time Jane Austen's great-grandmother was widowed and became the Master's housekeeper at the school. Her four sons were given free tuition, all joining the rising professional class: two surgeons, an apothecary, and Francis Austen, the lawyer. Free tuition was a rare commodity; perhaps less than a fifth of the school's 50 or so pupils were local free students, the remainder being fee paying boarders who came with the Master when he was appointed.

The new climate of religious tolerance now allowed non-conformist chapels to be built. The first was in Bessels Green (1716), and was followed by other chapels in Sevenoaks. The first Baptist chapel was built in 1754 behind the west side of London Road, and would have had a tank to allow for the total immersion of new converts. The Wesleyans meanwhile had a small chapel behind a shop on the east side of the High Street, given to them by Mrs. George the owner, a friend of the Wesley brothers. They often visited the area, preaching at Shoreham church in 1744, where the Reverend Vincent Perronet, an exceptional man of Huguenot descent, saw them as an integral part of the Church of England, and was in turn called by the Wesleys 'the Archbishop of Methodism'. They also preached in an 'open place near the Free School', presumably the upper High Street outside the school, in 1746, and on other occasions at the Vine.

The first cricket match ever to be reported in the national newspapers was played on the Vine in 1734, although the game had almost certainly

70 The 1636 bridge at Longford, near Dunton Green, with the mill on the left of the picture (part of the arched opening through which the Darent flowed is visible).

been played there for some time before. The Archbishop's vineyard had long since disappeared and the use of the site for cricket must have been due to John Sackville, the second son of the 1st Duke of Dorset, whose family owned the Vine. He organised the match against the Sussex team, captained by Viscount Gage, perhaps as an opportunity for a sporting wager.

Long distance travel was still very difficult due to the fragmentation of responsibility among parishes. Cromwell's Commonwealth had attempted to create a national system of road mending but without success, and the growth in traffic prompted the development of the turnpike system which allowed private enterprise to maintain or build a length of road of prescribed width, materials and drainage, and to charge a toll to users. The first Turnpike Act in Kent was in 1709 for 'repairing and amending the highways leading from Seven Oaks to Woods Gate and Tunbridge Wells', starting at Riverhill. The road would have been particularly awful in winter as it crossed the Low Weald and Medway, and its importance for access to the new spa town was

matched by its importance as the Rye fish route (whose carriers were partially exempt from tolls from 1761 on) and as a post road.

It was 40 years before the adjoining stretch to the north, from Sevenoaks to Farnborough, was covered by a separate Turnpike Act (1749). This followed the roads through Sevenoaks, Riverhead, Dunton Green and up Star Hill (previously called Morants Court Hill) to Knockholt Pound, and then linked up with an earlier turnpike from Farnborough to Lewisham, making Sevenoaks considerably more accessible to London. Turnpikes tended to be carried out in a piecemeal fashion since they were mainly created and funded by local entrepreneurs. Local labour was used to build them, and John Brampton wrote to the Countess Stanhope about a Chevening man working on the turnpike between Riverhead and Seal in late 1766. Only the year before, in May 1765, he had written, 'we have had great talke of a new Turnpike Road from Godstone to Rootham and I here say to Dartford which will come through Westerham Brasted Sunderidge and the Backside of Chipstead to Riverhead which

71 Chipstead Square's mostly Victorian buildings (seen in the early 1900s) show that prosperity recovered after the decline in ripier traffic which had passed through the village. On the right is the *Crown* public house offering Westerham Ales from the Black Eagle Brewery.

Chipstead people are much Displeased at as it does not go through their street but I sopose was put by, by Mr. Polly, but I here there is an Act of Parliament past for the Road and to began immediately'. He assumes Mr Polly, or Polhill, of Chipstead Place was responsible for diverting the road through Bessels Green, but it may have been the thought of negotiating Chipstead Hill that had influenced the route.

The Godstone to Wrotham turnpike of 1765 improved the east-to-west journey to a far greater extent. The north-south turnpikes had largely followed the existing roadways, which were originally Saxon drove roads to the Wealden outback and which followed the shortest route downhill. A short section of one of these survives in the grounds of Riverhill House, bypassed during the building of the first turnpike in 1710 to provide a shallower gradient and the bends necessary to slow the carriages.

The original east-west road in Holmesdale, however, running against the grain of the county, had followed the narrow strip between the river Darent flood terraces and the sometimes deeply cut dry river valleys of the rising Chartland. It

was not until 1679 that a Chevening estate map showed a road from Brasted to Westerham or Sundridge, while the Riverhead to Seal section usually went via Sevenoaks Vine, at least for carriages, in the late 17th century.

Army map makers, who were reconnoitring the route in November 1755 in connection with possible troop movements, found the 'high Road' a sandy track eight to nine feet (2.4 to 2.7m.) wide, flooded either side of Westerham and up to Sundridge. The words 'high road' suggest one or more lower tracks possibly used only in summer. They by-passed the equally bad stretch from Riverhead to Seal, and camped on Sevenoaks Common, proposing a future camp around the Windmill there. From there, they recommended either the Locks Bottom road (the old river valley road now called Seal Hollow Road) to Seal, or crossing the south part of Knole Park to pick up the road to Stone Street and Ightham. The new turnpike a decade later also frequently struck out on its own line, taking, for example, a new line east of Seal to miss out Styants Bottom and running round the south side of Oldbury Hill to avoid the old route up the old Iron-Age ramparts.

Contemporary maps show various toll gates, called 'turnpikes', at the bottom of Riverhill and north of Longford Bridge (on the London to Rye road), and west of Bessels Green at the Chevening road junction, west of Bat and Ball, and west of Seal at the Seal Hollow Road junction (these three on the Godstone to Wrotham road). Most would have had toll houses or cottages adjacent, and Frank Richards, writing in 1901, records tollkeepers' cottages surviving in Dunton Green and Seal, the latter with the Marquess of Camden's arms on it.

The road down the Darent Valley north from Otford had switched banks at intervals during its history, probably due to local flooding and the meandering river. The earlier route, on the east side of the river, probably went straight from the west side of the green facing Otford Church, north to Preston Farm, and along the east side of Shoreham Church following the farm track called Park Lane. Anthony Stoyel believes that this may have been superseded by the irregular higher road shown by Hasted (on his map of the Hundred of Codsheath, 1778), as the row of tightly packed 17th-century cottages facing Park Lane until 1935 would have precluded even an alley passing through. Hasted's map also shows the 1766 turnpike road running around the south and east sides of Otford's square green, then going east to meet the twisting road to reach Shoreham Church. Further down the valley, a toll cottage survives at 5 Riverside, Eynsford, also called Toll Bar

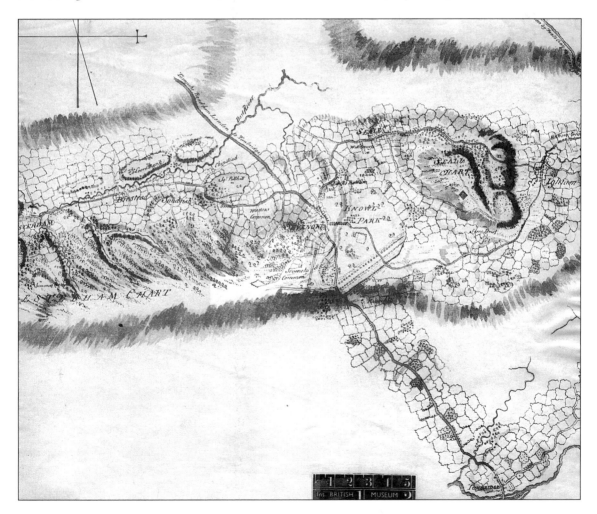

72 Colonel Watson's map of 1755 shows the difficulty of the west-to-east route, with no direct road shown between Riverhead and Seal.

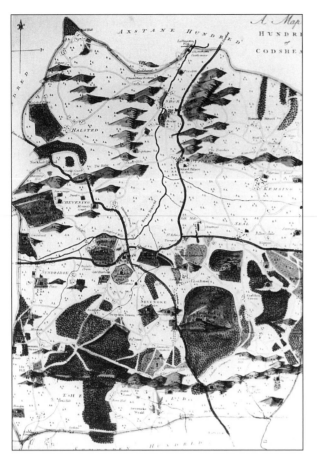

73 The 1778 map of the Hundred of Codsheath accompanied Hasted's *History and Topography of Kent*, a work which has thrown light on the early development of Holmesdale by its record of the balances of power among secular and church estates.

Cottage, which was built in the 16th century. Sparepenny Lane, on the west side of the valley, was, as its name suggests, an alternative to the turnpike road. An early drier route to Dartford by-passed this upper Darent section by going down Seal Hollow Road, across Steadles or Stiddolphs Heath to join Child's Bridge Lane from Seal, up the Downs to Romney Street and then down to Eynsford by one of the most beautiful roads in Kent.

Sir Walter Stirling's plan for a turnpike from Shoreham to Green Street Green and Bromley had already won parliamentary approval in 1810, when it was discovered that he had not got the agreement of all the landowners involved, including the small freeholders of the cottages facing

the Darent bridge at Shoreham. The Act was repealed the following year, but the broken roofline of the cottages shows where one had already been pulled down in readiness for the new road. The road was never built, and 20 years later the new turnpike up Polhill became the main route to London. Stirling, a newcomer to Shoreham in 1805, clearly had had great local ambitions, although they were never really fulfilled. He had already demolished some old buildings between the *George* inn and New House to enclose a 'pleasure garden' on the site of the late Shoreham House, and then had built a family pew for himself over the rood loft in the church. He never, however, filled the position locally that families like the Polhills had or the Mildmays would.

Many landowners undertook road diversions, either to improve their views and vistas, or merely to move roads which ran straight past the fronts of their homes, as at Sevenoaks Park (the site of Park Grange) in the late 17th century. In the late 18th century a spate of changes appear to have been prompted by Chevening's substantial road alterations in 1785. In 1791 Dr Turton of Brasted Place moved the Ide Hill road further east from its junction with the main road at the site of the present lodge, while at Combe Bank the relocated road was made possible by Lord Stanhope's new road to Sundridge. The Polhills had probably already transformed the Chipstead to Riverhead road into a private drive, and it so appears on a map of 1765. This pattern continued in the early 19th century, when the Streatfeilds closed off the village street in Chiddingstone to create a lake for their Castle.

The emparkment process enclosed common land. Common rights of access for certain purposes were frequently ignored and it was only where adjoining landowners such as Lords Stanhope and Amherst were competing for the same piece of common, as at Chipstead, that the process was brought to a halt. Knole Park grew from 446 acres in 1565 to 928 acres in 1929 by a series of piecemeal additions, one of which, in 1724, added 93 acres of Julians Common to the south end. The four freeholders who had nominal ownership over it sold their interest for £210, and were probably glad that a haunt for highwaymen and vagabonds would now be brought under

74 Knole's ice house still exists to the west of the house. Here it is being stocked up in winter with ice, perhaps cut from the several ponds in the park. Most of the major houses in the 18th century, including Chevening and Combe Bank, would have had an ice house.

75 The southern pair of entry lodges to Knole, sketched by the author's great-grandfather, Richard Rayner, on one of his summer strolls into Holmesdale in the 1870s.

76 This entrance lodge to Chipstead Place is more a dower house than a gatekeeper's residence. It survives at the top of Chipstead Hill, along with its Lutyensesque gate posts.

77 Percy Lodge, at the east entrance to Chipstead Place, appears to be later than its other lodges, dating from a partial emparkment of the common. The trees are now gone and the junction, off Witches Lane and Chipstead Lane, is much busier today.

78 Greatness House's thatched roofed lodge (now demolished) was probably the smallest lodge in the area.

79   One of the lodges of Wildernesse House, in Park Lane, Seal, before 1930.

control, although the commoners were not consulted about losing their rights.

A similar enclosure took place in 1803 when Lord Camden of Wildernesse enclosed the area of Stiddolph's Heath which now includes Hillingdon Avenue and made a new drive and entrance lodge to avoid the flooding of the dip in the Bat and Ball to Seal road by Millpond Wood. To do this, he sought and received the approval of four inhabitants of Greatness, who were presumably the only freeholders there and, as such, had a voice. In the process, Wildernesse gained an additional lodge, making six in total, though the lack of any resemblance between them suggests that they were built at different times, reflecting different priorities.

Old Ladd's Hill, a corruption of Old Lodge Hill, was the site of one of the earliest lodges of the archbishop's Little Park to the south of Otford. Lodges are derived from fortified entrances, an idea that works best with Knole's two sets of paired lodges. Those at the Plymouth Drive entrance are the most interesting architecturally, and probably oldest, but the split accommodation must have been difficult to use. The lodges would have

housed estate employees or retainers and their families, who would have opened and closed the gates on demand.

Lodges were also sometimes used like pawns, to lay claim to new areas of ground. Chipstead Place's Lodge at Witches Lane, Wildernesse's lodge near Bat and Ball, and Combe Bank's lodge in Brasted all fill this function. The latter seems very odd as it is in another village, but it may have been built as an alternative exit in case of flooding.

The architecture of lodges is interesting too, and follows prevailing styles from Chipstead Place's classical lodge to the north of the house, and the Gothic *cottage ornée* of Kippington Lodge, to the town's last lodge built in Oakhill Road in 1914 in fluent Arts and Crafts style. Usually they have more decorative detailing than a house, and compact, almost square plans, which the addition of a second storey can make almost into a cube. Being outlying and small, they have usually survived, even when the original house has disappeared, and this also applies to other outbuildings, such as stable blocks and gardeners' cottages. Their earlier links to a distant great house are often not

80   Kippington Lodge, photographed in the late 19th century, has since lost its rustic fence and gate.

recognised, though there is often a clue in their more picturesque qualities and architectural detailing, as in the case of the surviving gardeners' houses at Ashgrove and Kippington Court (in Windmill Road and Brittains Lane respectively), built in the late 19th and early 20th centuries. Boundary walls have often survived too, as at Chipstead Place, Montreal and Brasted Place, and become architectural features in their own right. Follies and other smaller structures have had greater problems, and thus Montreal's lovely little belvedere pavilion near Coldharbour is soon likely to fall down.

The next century would bring far greater changes than any previous ones. What we know of the old order owes a great deal to Hasted, writing in the 1790s, who took the county guide book to a new level in his many-volumed *History and Topographical Survey of Kent*. At first sight this is a 'who's who' of the county, giving potted family histories, but there are also records of relationships of power and dependency for manors, churches and other institutions which allow us to reach back to the origins of settlements in Holmesdale.

VI

Victorian Growth

Nineteenth-Century Sevenoaks

The Town

By the accession of Queen Victoria, in 1837, the old south end of Sevenoaks was more or less as we see it today. The Queen was welcomed to the throne more than perhaps any previous monarch, with a feast in the High Street and sporting events on the Vine.

It was shortly after this that the first overall map of Sevenoaks was made, the Tithe Map (1839) which, with the Tithe Apportionment Book, plotted the changes from a complex system of tithe collections to a money equivalent. While it shows both the roads and boundaries of land holdings, there is much less detail than on the first Ordnance Survey map of the town in 1870.

We know a great deal about this early part of the 19th century, before the arrival of the railway, thanks to Jane Edwards, who was 71 years old when she wrote her *Recollections and Conversations about Old Sevenoaks* in 1863. She wrote the book as a dialogue between an Aunt (herself) and her niece, Mary, a tiresome style, particularly as Mary's function seems to be to register alarm and wonder at appropriate moments, and to remind her aunt to take a little rest from time to time. There are other difficulties, too. Few of the buildings had recognisable names or numbers, and are identified only by their owners. She also largely ignores the cottages and lives of the very poor.

It is primarily a story of people: there are cautionary tales of young ladies like the niece of the Quinnells who danced too much at a ball, became overheated and died. Other young ladies made imprudent matches and suffered the consequences. Mrs. Wilmot, the doctor's wife, lived next door to the present-day Outrams, and with her children was regularly turned out of the house at midnight by her husband, and had to take refuge with her neighbours. Mrs. Staples patiently awaited the return of her husband from America. When she had heard of his death, she had gone into mourning. Later she heard that he was still alive and she had 'brightened up', beginning her long patient wait again – but he never did return. Disaster was never far away. A man living in London Road gave his epileptic wife gin, because the brandy recommended by the doctor was finished. He was horrified, however, when she died and the guilt drove him mad. Two husbands are recorded shooting themselves after the deaths of their wives, but one of these, a Mr. Claridge of Claridge House, was less to be pitied by Miss Edwards, as he had been 'haughty and reserved'.

At the same time there were touches of the absurd. The town's principal coach maker, who lived next to the White House in the Upper High Street, was a mixture of oaf and anarchist. He once rode a horse backwards to prove how easy it was to attract attention and win a bet. A favourite image is of him writing rude remarks on people's houses and turning around signs. His devout wife found that 'her husband was a great trial to her'.

Several elderly people who were admitted to the almshouses near Sevenoaks School are all described as good, respectable people, suggesting that the almshouses were in practice restricted to the middle classes. Her only reference to the workhouse was a description of a 'very bad woman' who 'told fortunes', under the cover of taking in washing, who had lived in a cottage along an alley to the south of the White House.

The Duchess of Dorset, widow of the 3rd Duke, appears in several references, such as when she condescended to allow the Lambarde daughters of Park Place to walk with her children in Knole. She bestowed her favour on certain others in the town, appointing one her librarian, another her almoner, and was instrumental in getting some of the elderly into an almshouse. Her son, the young Duke of Dorset, meanwhile, visited an Irish family in the tiny cottage beside Cage Pond (66 High Street) and left a gold seven shilling piece in the old Irishman's snuffbox. (Frank Richards has a variation of this obviously legendary story, identifying a different house and with a sovereign being pressed into the old man's palm.) The Duke himself died tragically in 1815 when his horse fell on him after jumping a stone wall near Dublin.

By following Jane Edwards's tour, starting at the south end of town, we can lament with her the partial demolition of the Lambardes' former house, Park Place. Park Grange, the present house (now a part of Sevenoaks School), was not built here until the mid-1860s. Park Place had been rebuilt around 1789, probably in stone, and a contemporary engraving shows that it had a slightly awkward appearance, with two tall thin projections at each end of the main elevation, and large Venetian or Palladian windows under a central pediment. The house was sold to Colonel Thomas Austen when the Lambardes moved to Beechmont in 1841, and he pulled down much of it.

Moving northward, past a blacksmith's forge, we come to the *Royal Oak* (originally the *Black Bull*), which had been refronted in its present ragstone around 1820. There had been a long room projecting into the street beyond (sometimes used for balls), which had been known as the Officers' Room in the Napoleonic wars when the army was quartered there.

Then came the late medieval hall house of which the Old Post Office is now part, which at some stage had been divided into three separate dwellings. It has some 18th- and 19th-century sliding windows, a cheaper alternative to sash or

81   A refreshment break at the *Royal Oak Hotel* during the transportation by A.A. members of a battalion of Guards from London to Hastings on 17 March 1909. The chosen route passed through Sevenoaks, and the town had never seen so many cars at once before.

82 The Old Post Office in the upper High Street has had two types of decorative tile-hanging added later to conceal its timber frame. Mr. Wood, the shop's owner, poses outside with his daughter Louise, *c*.1919.

83 The medieval building at Raley's corner, *c*.1920, looking north to the town centre.

casement windows. The Chantry adjacent is a substantial brick house built around 1700, either on the site of the original chantry priests' dwelling, or on the land that supported them. Its stable buildings to the south would be built in 1905, the hay loft door and its roof overhang on brackets soon to be made redundant by the motor car.

The almshouses and grammar school opposite had changed little since they had been built in the 1720s. Miss Edwards recalls King George III passing through Sevenoaks on his way to Tunbridge Wells, and stopping to allow the headmaster to kneel on a cushion outside the carriage door and converse with him. Manor House, next door, had been built in the late 18th century by the 3rd Duke of Dorset for a Captain Coast in guilt at having ruined him at cards. It has a coursed ragstone facade, but with cheaper random ragstone sides and is on the site of the medieval *New Inn*, bought by Archbishop Bourchier in 1481. The next property to the north used to be the Sherriff's Office, and had a strong room at the back for prisoners.

The Old Vicarage opposite, built in the early 18th century, was no longer required for vicars standing in for absentee rectors – the Rectory itself, set back from the roadway had recently been replaced with a Gothic revival house, a style Miss Edwards called 'Elizabethan'. The majority of people at this end of the town seem prosperous, and include attorneys, clergymen and school masters. A number of inns dating from the heyday of the market had been converted to

85 The White House, Sevenoaks in December 1971, shortly before its demolition. The fairly ill-proportioned facade concealed an earlier building behind.

private houses; the less than salubrious *Three Cats Inn* had been replaced by New House (built *c*.1728), and the *Six Bells* had been a private house for the previous 70 years. Six Bells Lane had been renamed Parsonage Lane, though it has now reverted to its original name.

The White House (now demolished) may have originally been Tudor, but was largely rebuilt in 1840, its name complementing the Red House opposite. Its facade was ungainly and out of proportion to its surroundings, but it had retained a Tudor fireplace and presumably contemporary timber framing. There were supposed to be secret tunnels from here to the church – on one occasion a bullock got into them. On the east side of the High Street (outside No.66, the modern Waitrose) was Cage Pond, which had probably been dug for the livestock that were brought to market, a forerunner of the horse trough. An etching of 1828 shows it with a fence on three sides, but Miss Edwards remembers it with 'willow pollards, docks, mallows, and nettles', 20 years earlier. By the mid-1840s the pond had been filled in, and the surrounding fence removed, as the town was tidied up. Frank Richards calls it the Town Pond, with the weighbridge beside it for assessing tolls on vehicles. The Old Cage was at the junction of the High Street and London Road, a highly visible and public location. The cage cost £16 to build in 1714, and must have been very small and basic.

84 Raley's corner and the top of Six Bells Lane in the mid-19th century, showing the medieval continuous-jetty house (31-37 High Street). This would have its framing concealed by render and weatherboard in the next few decades, and at the same time the present distinctive gables would be added. The two buildings at the left would be demolished when Temple House was built in 1884.

86 The Sevenoaks Coffee Tavern, later the West End Dairy, at the road junction around 1900. The facade of Outrams, the Archbishop's Reeve's house, leans out on the left, while to the right of the fountain all of the buildings have since been replaced.

87 The entrance to the West End Dairy (replaced by Midland Bank in 1924) pictured around 1920 with its cheerful proprietor.

Oddfellows Hall (behind Nos.1-5 London Road), used to be called the Coffee House or Old Assembly Rooms. It had the largest room in the town which was used by the gentry for balls and political meetings. While St Nicholas's church was being repaired in 1812 it was used for services, though marriages and christenings had to be at the nearest parish church. The Baptists and Methodists also used it, and John Wesley preached in a long room in the yard which was also used as an auction room. The *Chequers* opposite is mentioned in the context of London Road, as though its main entrance was on that side at that time.

Around 1800, the *Crown Hotel* (demolished earlier this century and on whose site the Stag

88 An early view, around 1860, of the *Royal Crown Hotel* and the backs of the *Chequers*, looking down London Road. The hotel looks a more interesting building here, in its pre-embellishment phase; however, the road-crossing hotel sign mentioned by Jane Edwards had already gone.

89 The *Royal Crown Hotel* (site of the Stag Theatre and Post Office) in the 1920s.

Theatre and the Post Office now stand) was the best inn in town. It had a large beam spanning London Road, with a suspended Crown sign which swung in the wind, and across which one night a sleepwalker is said to have walked. The three owners since that time had each altered and improved it, the latest laying out the extensive gardens to the west. It was at the *Crown* in 1859 that the Volunteer Movement was formed, with Multon Lambarde as its first officer. They later drilled in 'Mr Bligh's spacious drying house' in the High Street.

90 Looking up London Road from South Park around 1920. The signage of Uridge's seems to have been touched up for the postcard.

Brands Lane was about to be demolished as Miss Edwards was writing. Originally a farm track leading across fields to Kippington, it had become built up on both sides, creating a long narrow alley whose tightly packed nature made it 'malodorous and pestilential'. Here tenements were tightly packed, with old farm outhouses and subdivided, possibly medieval, buildings alongside newly built cottages. There was a well, but the density of occupation must have made the water quality doubtful. Buildings on its south side were demolished when it was widened to form South Park. Among the buildings lost were the stables next to the *Royal Oak*, which were actually part of the *Bull* inn opposite, also known at various times as the *Pied Bull* and *Swan*, and now the *Dorset Arms*. A sketch plan drawn in 1765, when the *Bull* was sold by Erasmus Maddox, shows the inn extending up to Dorset Street, where it had a tiny garden. It was in a doorway here that one of the last of the King's men was killed after the Battle of Solefields.

The first Baptist chapel, behind No.31 London Road, was built in 1754, and had a light blue dome with a lead cornice surround and a chandelier below it, directly above the central Baptistry. The first minister was Michael Bligh who served for over 40 years, but his successor was considered too liberal, despite the success of

91 This little shop in Lime Tree Walk points back to the market stall origin of many of the town's shops.

92 The entrance to the Shambles around 1865, seen from London Road. The small Kentish mansard-roofed butcher's shop is still in use as such, although the adjoining building (no.18) has been replaced, and the *Dorset Arms* on the opposite side is unrecognisable today.

93 Vallin's shop before 1910 displaying some valuable bananas and attractively priced strawberries. Just to the left can be seen the ivy-covered facade of Lady Boswell's School, built in 1818.

94 W. Knight's 1864 drawing of Walnut Tree House, or Pump House, at London Road's north entry into town, shows both tree and pump, and a very interesting house, now sadly lost. The building may be a cross-winged hall house. A culvert marks the start of an open drain running below it.

95 Albert Turner's *c.*1870 sketch of Knott's smock mill in Eardley Road, demolished around 1890. The artist lived in nearby Mill Cottage on Tub's Hill.

his wife's Sunday School, and was forced to leave. Meanwhile, a General Baptist chapel, also in London Road just to the north, replaced a subdivided medieval house, and was later used as a Literary and Scientific Institution.

At the north end of London Road was the Pump House or Walnut Tree House, a tall house of great character (on the site of the present Swiss Life Offices). An engraving by W. Knight shows the tall public water pump outside, what appear to be a sweep of steps up to the south side entrance and a medieval cross wing, and of course, the walnut tree. The 1870 Ordnance Survey shows it on a much deeper and more irregular plot than other properties to the south, as though it were the original farm out of whose lands much of the west side of London Road had been carved.

Below this was Knott's windmill, a weatherboarded smock mill that would be pulled down around 1890 and become the garden of No.25

96 The north end of the High Street seen from the front of *Bligh's Hotel* around 1920.

97 *(left)* The north end of *Bligh's*, then Bethlehem Farm (photographed *c.*1875), with a cluster of farm buildings and, behind, a large barn and pair of oast houses facing onto Pembroke Road.

98 *(above)* *Bligh's Hotel* and the lower High Street around 1900.

99 119-123 High Street (*c.*1875), showing the shops of Mr. Gandy, saddler and harness maker, and Amos Pett, basket maker. The uneven roof lines may indicate older properties which have been refaced. At the far right is the end of Bligh's farm wall and the entrance to Brewery Lane.

Eardley Road. The 1870 Ordnance Survey shows it in an open area, but with Eardley and Gordon Roads ominously dotted on. The windmill on Sevenoaks Common had already gone by then (although it appears on the 1839 map), and a ragstone cottage had been built blocking its perfectly shaped south-facing wind funnel. Sevenoaks Weald's windmill on the south side of the green is shown on the 1870 map, while the smock mill at Bassett's Hill, south-east of Ide Hill, had only just closed that year, another victim of the new large steam mills.

The central area between the High Street and London Road (also called the Back Street) was called the Middle Row, and contained the 'old Bedlam' or Bethlehem Hospital (now *Bligh's Hotel*), an asylum for the insane until 1828. This had been rented by the original Bethlehem Hospital in Moorfields as supplementary accommodation, as it had large gardens for patients to walk in. The new owner, a Mr. Bligh, was beginning to let rooms in Jane Edwards's time. She gives its original name as St Botolph, a name which must date back to its purchase by the vestry

of St Botolph's Without, Bishopsgate in 1646. Its lands stretched from Bank Street (then called Black Boy Lane) to Hitchen Hatch Lane, covering the whole central area between London Road and the High Street/Dartford Road. Frank Richards refers to a girder within the old house with a date of 1206 on it, but this seems far too early and may be a misreading of a carpenter's mark. Miss Edwards also recalls an old draw well at the

100 Smith's Suffolk Place brewery in the lower High Street in the early 1900s, later replaced by the Electric Cinema.

101 Suffolk Terrace, by the entrance to present-day Suffolk Way, on the eve of the construction of the Electric Cinema (later the Granada) in the early 1920s.

102   The run of buildings (*c.*1860) from Bank Street up to *Bligh's Hotel* (far right) has now totally gone, including this farrier's forge, under whose canopy can be seen older timber framing with brick infill. Next door, *Holmesdale Tavern's* two bars can be identified from their ornate door canopies.

edge of the High Street nearby which had a large elm tree shading it. This appears on the 1839 Tithe Map but was later removed, and the tree was cut down to widen the road.

Almost opposite, on the east side of the High Street, stood Lord Suffolk's large late 18th-century house. After his death the old mansion was re-placed with six houses called Suffolk Place and later Suffolk Terrace, and the stables became a brewery. Nowadays, only the road, Suffolk Way, retains the name. The adjoining house to the south began life as a barn, and was then upgraded, first to a farmhouse, then a doctor's house and finally the London and County Bank. A similar story can be told of Growing Cottage, whose location at the north end of the town is unknown—possibly near Covell's farm, north west of Walnut Tree House. This began as a market butcher's stall, 3.5m. square, and latticed around with a single

103   Miss Hensman's sketch of nos. 113-117 High Street prior to their demolition around 1929. The right half was Corke's bookshop, the left, Miss Norris's restaurant, abutting the *Holmesdale Tavern*. The apparently shallow plan form suggests an 18th-century date. The bay window seems to have been an earlier form of shop front in Sevenoaks before plate glass became widely available.

104 This is believed to show a patriotic procession in the lower High Street around 1901, prompted perhaps by King Edward VII's accession or a victory in the Boer War. The buildings behind had been largely replaced by the 1930s, and their successors have themselves since been lost in the formation of Buckhurst Avenue and the rebuilding to its south.

105 The last days of Martin and Dolton's shop prior to its demolition to make way for Woolworth's. The bunting may be to celebrate King George VI's coronation in 1937.

106 The Market House around 1960, when it was in use as a public convenience.

107 Bank Street just after the Second World War, looking towards the 1843 Market House. The *Black Boy* pub faces the ragstone former Wesleyan Chapel.

108 The shop front display of World's Stores (72 High Street) in 1917 shows how plate glass shop fronts must have revolutionised shopping since their introduction in the previous century.

109 The *Rose and Crown Hotel* around 1920 (demolished *c*.1936, its decline possibly hastened by the relocation of the market in 1925). The buildings to the south with their fake stonework bays survive, but the buildings opposite (to the north of Lloyds Bank) were lost in the 1960s.

doorway. A Sevenoaks butcher, Mr. Covell, had transported it from Dartford, added boarding and a window, and then let it to a former employee. Over the years he kept enlarging it until it became 'quite a nice little place'. Another old barn, at the rear of Buckhurst Lodge, was used for theatrical performances, including one given by the great 19th-century actor, Edmund Kean.

Miss Edwards is less interested in the commercial heart of the town, although she offers tantalising glimpses, such as of Mr. Hodsell and his daughter who had a shop on the corner of Bank Street and the High Street (now Plaxtol Bakery). The father had a saddle shop facing the market house, while his daughter had a stationery shop and lending library facing the High Street. The ragstone Wesleyan chapel (now partly a pizza restaurant) in Bank Street had been built in 1853, facing the *Black Boy* public house, named after the Blackboy family.

According to Frank Richards the old octagonal market house still had its open ground storey at the start of the 19th century, but then was glazed in, which may have helped to stabilise it. In 1790 the Hundred Court instructed that it be repaired without delay as its condition was such as to 'endanger His Majesty's subjects in passing and repassing under the said building to buy and sell corn'. Its ornamental gables had also been cut off, perhaps at the same time, long before its demolition and replacement in 1843 by Earl Amherst of Knole for the sum of £309. The new building was open below, with an upper floor for the corn market and monthly County Court and Petty Sessions.

The annual fairs were still tremendous events, with drinking booths in the streets, and side shows. On one occasion there had been lions, and when one died the owners, banking on the fact most people would never have seen one before, replaced it with a Newfoundland bitch. A more serious side of the fair would have included the rows of female and male servants outside the present Lloyds Bank, waiting for inspection by potential employers. The fairs eventually ceased in the mid-1870s.

110 W. Knight's view of the High Street in the mid-19th century, looking towards the White House at the top of the hill. Bay projections are used as early shop windows in the days before plate glass. Pavements are marked by cobble edged gulleys.

The High Street seems to have undergone the greatest change and rebuilding in Miss Edwards's lifetime. There were still private houses like that next door to the *Rose and Crown* inn (which was on the site of 96 High Street, now the Iceland store), which had a white fence and honeysuckle climbing its front.

The town ended at the junction with Locks Bottom (now Seal Hollow) Road in those days, where large pine trees ran down alongside Knole's new boundary stone wall from Plymouth Drive to Blackhall, built by a team of Welshmen without mortar. There were some old cottages at the south and north ends of the Vine. Here the old two-storey weather-boarded Vine Pavilion on the present Vine Gardens had already been converted into cottages, before being replaced in 1850 by the present pavilion built by Earl Amherst of Knole.

Further north, along what is now Dartford Road, was the fir wood of Bradbourne on the left, and the paddock leading up to the grey ragstone frontage of Vine Court on the right. Owned by the Lambardes, this would later be the first of the large houses to fall to suburban housing. Mount Harry Road existed in part as a sheep track, Mount Harry being the name of the summer house of Henry Hughes of Bradbourne. The Bradbourne lands would have been quite well known as Mr. Hughes allowed public access. Further north, at the top of St John's Hill, a small nucleus was forming at Barrack Corner near the decaying militia barracks. The Congregational Church (now United Reformed Church) was built opposite it in 1865 and originally had an ungainly spire, which would be removed 15 years later when it was thought to be destabilising the whole structure.

111   The market place around 1912. Lloyds Bank occupies a former private house, later to be replaced by the present building.

112   Redman's Place, the alley between 78 and 80 High Street (now Lorimers and Barclays Bank) seen here around 1900. The mainly timber-framed houses have now gone, as has the first Wesleyan chapel in town, further to the east.

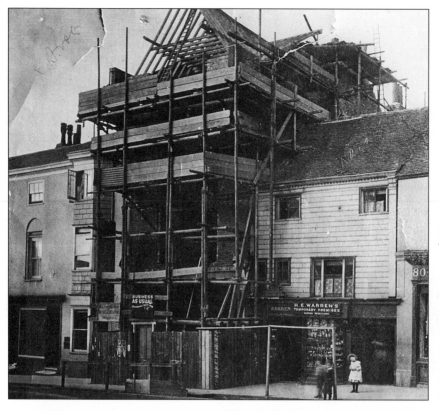

113 *(top left)* H.Warren's (84 High Street—now Brewers) jewellery shop's rebuilding in 1903 necessitated a move to temporary premises next door. The temporary premises, a timber-frame building, has since been replaced by a neo-classical building (occupied by Leslie Warren, Opticians, started by the son of the jeweller). The timber scaffolding would give today's Health and Safety inspectors some sleepless nights.

114 *(bottom left)* The aftermath of an 1894 fire at Mr. Dray's, in one of the upper High Street alleys (near present-day Waitrose). Given the timber frames of the adjoining two buildings, it was lucky that the fire damage was not more extensive.

115 *(top right)* The elegant Vine bandstand was given to the town in 1906 by Mr. Swanzy and here shelters some Edwardian ladies on a warm summer day. Beyond the elm trees is the 1886 Baptist church.

116 *(bottom right)* The peaceful south-west corner of the Vine, *c.*1900, with buildings in Dartford Road beyond.

117 The parade of shops on Dartford Road (seen *c*.1900) grew up to serve the new houses of Vine Court Road and Hitchen Hatch Lane. Their gable-ended design imitates the slightly earlier shops about half a mile to the north of the Hollybush Lane junction.

The Great Houses

At Knole the line of the Dukes of Dorset had ended in 1843 with the death of the 5th Duke, Charles Sackville-Germain. The house passed to Mary, sister of the 4th Duke, whose second husband was William Pitt Amherst, 1st Earl Amherst, and for a while Knole and Montreal were in the same hands. Mary's sister, Elizabeth, inherited in 1864, and through her husband, George West, 5th Earl de la Warr, the Sackville-West dynasty was formed. Mortimer, her fourth son, the 1st Lord Sackville, came to Knole in 1876 when his surviving older brother left to take over the de la Warr estates. In 1884 he restricted public access across the Park, and what might have passed without comment a century before was now unacceptable to a town which had begun to see itself in a much wider context. The public protest generated by the Knole Bridleway Dispute was mostly civilised, but when a crowd burned the new gate in front of the

118 *(top right)* The aftermath of Knole's great barn fire in 1887, viewed from the Kitchen Court on the east side. Firemen's water sprays have been scratched on to the negative to give the picture greater dramatic effect.

119 *(bottom right)* The homecoming of Lord and Lady Sackville in 1910 following the dismissal of the late Lord's illegitimate son's claim to the estate. The welcoming crowd wait outside the Manor House, then not yet part of Sevenoaks School.

house and broke some of its windows it was perhaps the final straw, and Mortimer left Knole for Scarborough, never to return. His investment in providing an independent water supply for Knole saved the day in August 1887 when a tremendous fire started in the medieval barn to the north of the house. The water came from a well in Weald Road where some ragstone retainers' cottages survive, owned until recently by the Knole Estates, although the little brick pumping station covered with creeper has gone in the last decade. Mortimer's brother, Lionel, inherited Knole in 1888, bringing with him his daughter

The home-coming of Lord & Lady Sackville.

120 The Laundry and Staff Garden at Knole around the turn of the century.

Victoria. Pepita, her late mother, had been the love of Lionel's life but they had been unable to marry, yet uncharacteristically British and American society accepted Victoria without reserve when Lionel was British Minister in Washington. She married her cousin, another Lionel and the next heir to Knole, in the chapel there in 1890.

Ashgrove (later West Heath School) dates from the early 19th century, although an earlier house had existed out on the common since the 1760s, built by Captain John Smith. He was a friend of Lord George Sackville, and is also credited with building the Bird House and artificial ruins to the east of Knole House. The original house looks very small on Andrews and Drury's map of 1769 and did not merit a separate entry in Hasted's description of the town. The new house, however, had a Classical grey brick east end, designed by Basevi in the late 1820s for William Haldimand. Some original marble fireplaces have survived from this although the grand central staircase, its deeply moulded ceiling and the oak panelling to surrounding rooms are said to be early 20th-century neo-Jacobean (they are

nicely done, although the architect is unknown). A dull brick Gothic central block, of different age, and a very relaxed stable west end completes the complex, and the latter includes a cobbled yard and a timber louvred clocktower on a low castellated tower.

The other major 19th-century house was Beechmont, which was built for Multon Lambarde in the 1840s (it is shown on the 1839 tithe map). Sited on the greensand ridge, at the edge of the common, to take advantage of the view, it may have been built on the site of an old hunting lodge. This house grew into a fairly unattractive Gothic pile, and became a boys' preparatory school in 1906 when Multon's son, William, moved to Bradbourne. The Lambardes had moved from Park Place to Beechmont and then on to Bradbourne within 70 years – an unusual degree of mobility. Both of these houses are unusual in taking up new sites and estates. Beechmont's choice of a site with a view was echoed by St Julians (1830) and the preposterous Weardale Manor (1906) at Toys Hill (now National Trust woodland).

121 The rear elevation of Ashgrove, later West Heath School, with the slightly later Gothic and modern extensions beyond.

122 Beechmont's upper lawn in the early years of this century when it was a boys' school. The monkey puzzle tree at the right of the picture survives on the ridge crest to the east.

123 Lord Hillingdon's major extensions at Wildernesse transformed it from a country house with a certain rustic charm into this anonymous complex, adding balustraded parapets and towering chimneys at the same time.

Many other houses underwent substantial rebuilding in the 19th century, including Wildernesse. An earlier house had been built in 1669 by Sir Charles Bickerstaffe with a substantial park around it, perhaps on the site of the medieval manor of Stiddolphs. John Pratt, the future Marquess of Camden, had the house remodelled and enlarged around 1800 by the architect George Dance, adding a third storey in the same squared ragstone blocks. The next phase of rebuilding and extension followed the purchase of the estate in 1884 by Sir Charles Henry Mills (later Lord Hillingdon), a banker who had previously rented it, who enlarged the house to about twice its original size.

The story was similar at St Clere, which had been bought by the Evelyn family in 1719. This had required substantial rebuilding at the time, including the stair, the roof parapet and the pine panelling, due to the frugality of the previous owner, Sir Charles Sidley. The Evelyns finally sold it in the 1870s to Sir Mark Collet, the Governor of the Bank of England. His alterations were less substantial but included an entrance porch, and a pair of entrance pavilions.

The increased size of families as child mortality decreased was responsible for some other major enlargements. Riverhill House, the home of the Rogers family since 1842, grew considerably in the 19th century to accommodate the growing family. Its hillside location led to linear growth, primarily to the east, although a drawing room was added at the west end, a copy of one in a cousin's house in Clapham. A large kitchen replaced the original one in the basement in 1900. It had a dairy below and a towering linen room above, and was 50m. or so from the dining room to avoid the cooking smells, but also resulted in cold food! The house was bought by John Rogers as a sheltered, lime-free home for his plant collection. He was a friend of Charles Darwin, who lived nearby at Downe, and he planted the bare slopes of Side Hilly Field above his house with large magnolias and rhododendrons from India and China. He also built the terraces which are now leaning drunkenly as solifluction tries to move them downhill. Inside the house there is Jacobean panelling saved from Stonepitts, Seal, in 1900, when it was removed by the tenant farmer's wife to eradicate rats.

Kippington, sold by the Austens to William James Thompson in 1865, was also greatly extended. The 1780 house was two-storey with parapets and dormers in the roof and to this was now added a three-storey block with lower ceiling heights to allow the parapets to line up. It may have been at the same time that the whole building was rendered, giving it a degree of unity.

The Victorian extension to the original Queen Anne house at Little Underriver (now Underriver House) did the opposite and provided higher ceilings in the new wing, where large new receptions rooms were added. The appearance of the original coursed ragstone was copied for the extension, but Victorian parsimony led to a much softer stone being used, which is now quite eroded.

Brasted Place's ugly 1871 extension by Alfred Waterhouse for William Tipping is a French Gothic folly, possibly inspired by Prince Louis Bonaparte's residence here in the 1840s. The future Emperor Napoleon III had carried out alterations to the original house during his stay, while also visiting the village with his pet eagle, and drilling his troops for his absurd invasion of France.

Knockholt House was demolished and rebuilt in 1890 by James Vavasseur, a silk merchant who had bought the property in 1863. Vavasseur was an old man at the time and probably designed the house himself. The completed building looked almost industrial, being extremely tall and rectangular, the parapets hiding its fully glazed roofs (which allowed the third floor to be an enormous winter garden). There was a peculiar tower 35m. high on one end with a conical section where all the chimney flues were brought together. The exterior was mostly rendered and painted white, and had rows of bullet-shaped lancet windows. Vavasseur's 'rather explosive' temperament and monumental vanity combined to create a building with no saving graces whatsoever, and which, worst of all, was near one of the highest points in Kent and highly visible. Surprisingly, it lasted until 1942 when it was sold for scrap, some of which, it is rumoured, formed part of the D-Day Mulberry harbours.

124 Knockholt House was designed by James Vavasseur for himself and reinforces the general view that he was a megalomaniac. The tower brought together the chimney flues and also, according to local tradition, had a boat alongside it for Vavasseur to ride out the next divinely ordained Flood.

125 Bulimba in Kippington Road, seen before its demolition in 1928, was a fine neo-Jacobean house. St Mary's Church is just behind.

126 Carrick Grange, seen shortly before its demolition in 1956 when it was being used as a maternity home, has the anonymous appearance of a municipal building, quite unlike its charming surviving lodge in Hitchen Hatch Lane.

127 Building workers pause during the construction of Vine Lodge in 1903. The aprons may signify master stonemasons or carpenters. The timber scaffolding poles behind are lashed together with perhaps greater care than modern-day scaffolders show.

At the same time, new large houses were being built on smaller plots within Sevenoaks. Properties like Kippington Grange (1874), Bulimba (1890), and Kippington Court (1900), all three along the new Kippington Road, Carrick Grange on Hitchen Hatch Lane, and Maywood (1874, later called Hatton House) on Bradbourne Road, were the new houses of wealthy commuters, city men willing to forgo large estates in order to be near the railway station. To accommodate all this new building, many of the older large houses were demolished, beginning with the mid 18th-century Vine Court in 1878 to make way for new houses in Vine Court Road.

The Railway Link

The first terminus in Sevenoaks was opened in June 1862 at Bat and Ball. There had been a link to Tonbridge via Redhill since 1842, and the long wait for a local connection had stirred up great anticipation. The first speculative housing developments were built in the St John's area in anticipation of a line along the valley, although other possible stations, including Riverhead

Square, had been considered at various times. Local landowners, led by Lord Amherst, had strongly supported the railway with the best motives in mind, and had helped to determine the route via Otford, Shoreham and Eynsford to join the London Chatham and Dover line at Swanley. The influence of landowners can be seen in the siting of Kemsing Station (opened in 1874) well away from the village, principally to give the owners of St Clere early warning of the arrival of trains.

For six years Bat and Ball was the only terminus for Sevenoaks and was where the Prince and Princess of Wales in 1866 and Queen Victoria in 1867 arrived on visits to Knole. On the first occasion the royal couple took a route through the town to allow the people of Sevenoaks to welcome them, whereas the Queen's visit to the elderly Earl and Countess de la Warr to offer condolences on the death of their daughter took the lower profile Plymouth Drive entrance.

The South Eastern railway line, from London to Tonbridge via Orpington, arrived at Sevenoaks (Tub's Hill) in March 1868. The gradients

128 Tub's Hill railway station in the 1920s. The original footbridge was later replaced with a higher one, before the major rebuilding of the later 1970s.

129 The 1884 railway accident at the Tub's Hill station, between two goods trains after a signalling error, resulted in the death of one driver and fireman. The original station buildings are visible at the left of the picture.

demanded that the engineers bypass the town itself, following instead the dry valley just to the west of the Sevenoaks ridge. The North Downs and the Greensand ridge, however, had to be tunnelled through, and rows of air vents, large brick chimneys, follow the lines of these tunnels, the variations in design indicating the different ages of the tunnels.

The conditions endured by the navvies drafted in to build these tunnels were even mentioned by Karl Marx in *Das Kapital*. Flooding from underground water was a major problem in 1864, which was solved by sinking a well by the tunnel vent in Oak Lane and pumping the water away to a reservoir. This became the town's first main water supply, replacing public and private wells and pumps, such as the one surviving in the old bakery courtyard in Six Bells Lane. The navvies had a temporary camp in Dunton Green as the pub name *The Miners' Arms* recalls, and many of them settled in the area, adding to the steadily growing population.

The town's population had grown from just over 2,000 in 1801 to nearly 5,000 in 1861, but this was due more to reduced mortality than incoming families. The railway, however, allowed a new type of resident who could work during the day in London but sleep in Sevenoaks, thus creating the 'dormitory town'. By 1871, the population was just under 6,000, rising to 8,000 by 1881, and just under 10,000 at the turn of the century.

The Age of the Benefactors

Many of these newcomers developed a tremendous warmth for Sevenoaks and became great benefactors to the town, providing new buildings and shaping institutions. Yet at the same time they were greatly involved in changing the character of the town that had first attracted them, both by enlarging and improving it.

W.J. Thompson, a tea-merchant and founder of the Sevenoaks Water Company, had bought Kippington from the Austen family in 1864 when the tunnel contractor who had been renting it went bankrupt. Thompson, together with Captain Germain of Vine Court, later developed Bradbourne Park and Mount Harry Roads. He gave the Drill Hall site in Argyle Road to the

130 Brasted railway station in 1972 after a decade of post-Beeching disuse. The station site and a good deal of the track are now covered by the M25.

town, built St Mary's Church, Kippington on his own estate following a dispute with the Rector of St Nicholas, and helped found the Cottage Hospital.

James Germain left Vine Court, which the Lambarde family demolished to make way for new houses, and in 1874 built a new home for himself called Maywood (now the Adult Education Centre in Bradbourne Road). He was a local Liberal politician and used fellow Liberal T.J. Jackson as his architect. Germain played a major part in improving local sanitation and was a leader in the Knole bridleway protests of 1884.

Sir Charles Mills, later Lord Hillingdon, was a banker who bought Wildernesse from the Camden family in 1886. He helped to establish the Vine Constitutional Club in 1890, and gave Seal its village hall and fire station. The importance to him of the railway station at Bat and Ball caused him to lay out a new drive to it, now followed by Hillingdon Avenue.

In the villages, too, there was an awareness of the changing orientation away from the county and Maidstone, and towards London via the railway. Sir Mark Collet of St Clere was Governor of the Bank of England in the 1870s, and chose Kemsing as his parish church, rather than Ightham, opening a new drive towards it. Kemsing would ultimately benefit from his gift of St Edith's village hall (1911) and the extended graveyard's crinkle crankle wall (1920s), both designed by Godfrey Pilkington.

The Jackson family, who came to Sevenoaks in 1867 and lived in Vine Cottage, were to have a profound effect on the town. In 1870 Emily Jackson was given the use of one of the Lambardes' nearby cottages on the Vine to nurse a young local girl with tuberculosis who had developed hip abscesses. The child eventually died, but Emily's work became known and more children were sent from London, until within five years she had 11 patients. In the following year, she rented and renovated a larger house next door to her home and made it her new hospital. Her father later bought the house and added a laundry and kitchen garden, but soon this, too, would be outgrown. A new purpose-built Hip Hospital with 45 beds off Eardley Road was funded by public subscription and designed by her brother Thomas. In 1902, she moved her patients and staff to the new building in a grand procession of prams and starched uniforms. Emily Jackson's hospital, built for £10,000, had several atypical design features: the angled wings and their curved Dutch gable ends, the steep roof with its mannerist alternation of dormer roofs, and the stark zipper-like quoins to windows and doors standing out against the rendered walls.

Thomas Jackson was a pupil of Sir George Gilbert Scott in the early 1860s and lived with his parents in Sevenoaks, later marrying Alice Lambarde. His most celebrated works were at Oxford and Cambridge Universities and the famous restoration of Winchester Cathedral, which earned him, uniquely for an architect, a baronetcy. At Lime Tree Walk, with his father's backing, he set out in the late 1870s to create a more mixed community to counteract the trend towards social segregation in the newly developed estates. The South Park and Granville Road area, now separated from Kippington estate by the railway line, were proposed for middle-class development, and it was into this that he inserted his 24 cottages for working men, adding a coffee house in 1882. Some of the details he used – the large dormers, the strange Dutch gables, the brick quoins to the windows – are almost ugly, but he

131   Emily Jackson's Hip Hospital, *c*.1905.

132 T.G. Jackson's Lime Tree Walk.

created a good balance between, on the one hand, unifying elements such as the arched tunnels through to rear gardens, and on the other, local variations such as the stepped roofs and the window variations. This gives the road an enduring character. The first occupants, who rented their cottages, included shop assistants and gardeners. The gardens opposite, adjoining the coffee house, were communal, since Jackson was aware of the limited gardens in poorer roads in the Hartslands and St John's part of town.

Henry Swaffield was another great benefactor. He came to the town in his forties and lived in Granville Road in a comparatively modest house. His most important gifts to the town were centred around the top of The Drive, and included the Methodist Church, the former Public Library, the Retreat (a modern form of almshouse), and Cornwall Hall, all built over a period from 1903 to 1906. His earlier works included the Bandstand on the Vine in 1894, followed by the Band Practice Room adjoining, eight years later, and he also refurbished the old

Market House as a Technical Institute in 1896. As a Methodist, he was following in the traditional interest of non-conformists in idealistic projects.

New Institutions

From 1832 onwards there were a number of national and local reforms which changed the character of Sevenoaks. The Reform Act of 1832 led to the first parliamentary representation for West Kent, and the beginning of the shift of local power away from the Vestry. In Sevenoaks, the Local Board from 1871 was the town's first elected body, taking over some of the Vestry's duties, with Multon Lambarde of Beechmont as its chairman. This was housed in new offices, with stables, in Argyle Road. In due course it was supplanted by the Urban and Rural District Councils under the 1894 Local Government Act, which were created further to improve health and welfare locally, including drainage and sanitation, housing construction and refuse collection.

In 1835 the Highways Act took responsibility away from individual parishes by bringing them, together with the turnpike roads, into the Sevenoaks Highway District, at the same time replacing with a new highway rate the previous system of statutory labour using the local unemployed. Metalled roads of stone, constructed following Macadam's principles, became more common in this period, improving access to the town.

The first gas works were built at the south end of Hartslands Road in 1838, and were supplying the town's first gas lights in 1840. They later moved to a larger site by the railway terminus at Bat and Ball and the original works became a laundry, then a garage and now offices. Street lighting reached the villages of Holmesdale much

133 The *Sevenoaks Chronicle* offices decorated for King George V's jubilee in 1935. The building partly spans the cobbled entrance to the old Post Office Yard (now all replaced by Waitrose).

later, coming to Otford in 1901 (using oil and gas). Electric light, however, did not arrive in Sevenoaks until 1913.

In the year of the first national census in 1841, Payne's *Sevenoaks Almanac* first appeared, listing local officials and later a complete list of residents, a particularly useful publication for the then rare newcomers. The *Sevenoaks Advertiser*, first published in 1840 – the year of the penny post – was soon followed by other newspapers in Westerham and Sevenoaks.

The county police force was formed in 1857, leading to the first Police Station being built near the Vine in 1864 (later the Registry of Births, Deaths and Marriages). The building cost £3,000 to erect, and is a good modest building with a large glazed lantern. In the parishes, arrangements were less clear and Shoreham was still appointing constables in the 1860s.

A pumped water supply was established during the construction of the Sevenoaks-Tonbridge railway tunnel, replacing the old wells and handpumps, and a number of ponds, some man made, which provided useful water for washing or livestock. These included Cage Pond in the High Street, those at the top of Hitchen Hatch Lane (presumably for the nearby animal pound), at the top of The Drive, at the east end of Solefields Road, at the bottom of Tub's Hill, and the one at the base of the steep section of Oak Lane which was well known for its drainage problems and was called 'Flowfields' in the winter when it was used for skating. The provision of water was less straightforward in the surrounding villages. In Otford in 1887 the villagers decided to provide their own piped water from the spring in the grounds of Moat Farm, helped by Henry Mildmay of Shoreham Place who paid for the materials and installation.

The Public Health Act of 1875 recognised the connection between poor sanitation and disease through pollution of wells and springs by nearby cesspits. Sewage rates helped to finance the new infrastructure of sewer pipes, though villages like Otford, which used sewage as a natural compost, resented having to pay these. Its neighbour Shoreham, however, joined the new sewer being built to Dartford following the sound guidance of the Reverend Cameron and Mr. Mildmay. In Sevenoaks the line of the earliest sewers can

134 The Post Office and Telephone Exchange in South Park seen around 1920. Previously the Post Office had been at 56 High Street (site of Waitrose), moving to the new building in 1897.

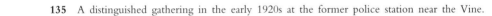

135 A distinguished gathering in the early 1920s at the former police station near the Vine.

136   The attractive Cottage Hospital of 1873 seen before its rebuilding in 1922 to form the present hospital.

be followed by means of the decorated cast iron vent pipes.

The Holmesdale Cottage Hospital was created in 1873 by voluntary subscription and had eight beds and a single nurse, assisted between 1892 and 1905 by Sir Joseph Lister, the pioneer of antiseptic surgery. There was a fever hospital at Sundridge for workhouse inmates, and other isolated or pest houses at Clenches Farm, Oak Lane (1874-1902), Fig Street (from 1902) and in earlier days at Starvecrow, Fawke Common, which dealt with smallpox and cholera. Nothing, however, catered for the general population. The Cottage Hospital was housed in an attractive building with a pair of projecting symmetrical end gables finished with decorative bargeboards, and a central vine-covered loggia, giving an appearance of something between a grand house and a superior railway station. Its 1922 replacement (the present hospital building) has none of the original character.

Schools

By the start of the 19th century the town had two charitable schools, Queen Elizabeth's Grammar School (now called Sevenoaks School) and Lady Boswell's School. The latter had been founded by Sir Ralph Bosville's daughter Margaret, who had married a distant cousin who spelt the family name Boswell. On her death in 1682, she had left an endowment for a school to teach 15 of the poorest children of the parish, and provide two scholarships of £12 per annum to Jesus College, Cambridge. The first known school building (now the Job Centre) was built on the Black Boy Garden in 1818, after new trustees had been appointed. This is an attractive building, the architect Cockerell's first commission, which has layers of dressed and undressed ragstone.

A growing concern for the moral and intellectual development of the poorer classes resulted in the early 1830s in the provision of public elementary schools. There were meant to be equal numbers nationally of National (Church of

England) and British (nonconformist) schools. In Shoreham, Humphrey St John Mildmay, J.P. paid for half the costs of the new 1833 National School, and continued to be involved with the School, though his appointment of the first teacher shows he regarded them very much as servants. Eynsford meanwhile had a British School, reflecting its strongly Baptist population.

Many villages already had schools; for example, Otford's National School developed out of its Sunday School. Ide Hill's first school started in 1809 in a private house, until a new school was built in 1855 by the eminent architect G.E. Street. Chipstead's first school of two rooms was apparently purpose-built in 1820, and the children had to pay 2d. a week for their tuition (the present school was built in 1895). Westerham's National School was built for £491 in 1828, and was away from the town in Hosey Hill. The school in London Road, Westerham was a second school, built in 1860, for girls and infants, while boys still had the uphill walk to Hosey Hill. Some villages were behind in all this; Kemsing's first school (now 17-19 St Edith's

Road) only started in 1847, six years after Chiddingstone's, while Crockham Hill had to wait till 1864. Many schools, like Shoreham's, were founded by prominent families. The Austens of Kippington founded St Nicholas's School on London Road (now a restaurant), nominated by Jane Edwards to receive the profits from the publication of her *Recollections*.

Victorian infants' schools built after the 1870 Education Act developed a design language of large Gothic windows, rooftop bellcotes or cupolas, and picturesque detailing that makes them instantly recognisable, even when they have since been converted. Ironically, one of the least successful in this sense is Thomas Jackson's 1872 Otford School.

During this period Sevenoaks School seems to have changed little. The south side of the original school building was raised in the 1870s, destroying the symmetry, in an effort to increase pupil numbers. The assembly hall and gymnasium followed in 1890. This was nothing compared with the major outlay at the new girls' school, Walthamstow Hall, in 1882. This was the

137 Seal Fire Brigade's inspection by the Duke of Kent in 1935 takes place in front of the village school. Seal Fire Brigade was formed around 1891 as a voluntary force.

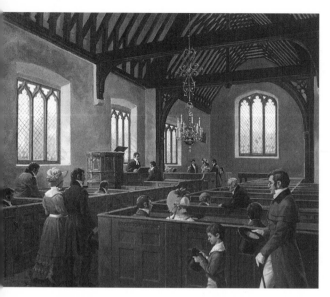

138 Derek Lucas's evocative painting tries to capture the character of Seal Church in the 1820s. The box pews are based on Ightham's surviving ones; however, the triple pulpit is speculative.

largest and most expensive (at £22,000) building in the town when it was built to house the School for Missionaries' Daughters which was being relocated from Walthamstow. The founder's daughter lived in Sevenoaks and had recommended this 'Kentish village' with its healthy air and open country.

In addition there were a great many small private schools, mostly for girls, which occupied existing houses. Westerham in the late 19th century had six of them, including one in General Wolfe's former home, Quebec House.

Churches

The Church of England in the 19th century underwent a great deal of internal conflict. On one side it was a wealthy and conservative institution and, like its churches, old and in need of urgent repair. Tithes were still collected until the early 1840s, when they were commuted to rents, and in the process Tithe maps, the first systematic mapping of parishes, were produced to help record the changes. At the same time forces of reform were at work. Old churches were repaired

139 St Nicholas' Church in 1862 showing the covered way at the east end.

140 *(above)*   The south approach to Riverhead, sketched by the author's great-grandfather Richard Rayner in the 1870s, showing Decimus Burton's church on the sandy knoll.

141 *(right)*   The ragstone Congregational Church at St John's Hill seen in the first 15 years of its life before its ugly, destabilising spire was removed in 1880.

and reordered, and new ones were established in the growing centres of population. New parish churches were generally founded by powerful or wealthy individuals, just as the earliest churches had been. The new churches at Sevenoaks Weald (1820) and Riverhead (1831) were founded by Multon Lambarde and Lord Amherst, who for the latter employed Decimus Burton, the architect of the Calverley development in Tunbridge Wells. St Lawrence, Seal Chart, was built in 1867–8 by the Wilkinson family of Frankfield in memory of their six-year-old daughter Mary Rachael who had died the year before.

Many older churches were in a poor state of repair. St Nicholas's was 'in such a ruinous condition that it is dangerous for the inhabitants to attend Divine Service', prompting an Act of Parliament in 1811 to allow the raising of funds. In the course of the repairs, crenellated battlements

142 The Congregational Church Hall in Hollybush Lane *c*.1900, with a large group perhaps celebrating the hall's opening amid a random scatter of scaffold poles. The north end of Vine Court Road appears relatively undeveloped at this time, judging by the open spaces beyond.

and high clerestory windows were added. The main phase of church restorations took place in the second half of the century, including Sundridge (1848), Otford (1862), Shoreham (1864), Brasted (1864), Chevening (1869), Kemsing (1870), St Nicholas, Sevenoaks (1878) and Westerham (1882). Many of these were particularly heavy handed and often involved major architects like Street at Sundridge and Otford and Waterhouse at Brasted (he subsequently extended Brasted Place in 1871).

Galleries and box pews were removed from many churches, as at St Nicholas, Shoreham, Otford, Kemsing and Westerham, the latter also losing its three-decker pulpit and early 19th-century plaster ceilings. St Nicholas's late Jacobean galleries had wrapped around three sides of the

church and together with the box pews must have made it very dark inside. Shoreham also lost Stirling's squire's gallery over the rood and Otford had a timber arcade (perhaps like that at Wingham, another of the Archbishop's manors) replaced in stone.

New Housing

The first major housing development was at Hartslands in the 1840s, when a 12-acre field was laid out as a working-class area. The result was quite impressive, with each road having its own character. Prospect Road is excitingly narrow and steep, Cobden Road has two sides of terraced housing, Bethel Road incorporates the odd, possibly older ragstone cottage, and Sandy Lane is

mostly terraced, but with less uniformity, and with a narrowing at the bottom end where the former laundry yard (present day Briar Cottage) projects into the road.

In the next two decades, the villas of St John's and the east end of Bradbourne were built, drawn by the magnet of the new Bat and Ball railway station. At this stage the pattern of the poorer north and wealthier south end that Thomas Jackson would deplore was not as established, the St John's area being still separated from the town by woods and paddocks. The workhouse had been

143 The west elevation of Vine Court by W. Knight, seen from Dartford Road, around the middle of the 19th century.

144 The lower end of Granville Road in the 1890s when the houses were quite new and a rural landscape stretched across to Polhill.

demolished, but the area was still called 'Gallows Common'.

The new housing of the 1870s and 1880s extended the town towards the new Tub's Hill railway station, and included Granville, Eardley and Argyle Roads. Another strand extended the High Street northwards, creating Dartford and Vine Court Roads. The lands between these two northwards extensions were inevitably filled in between 1890 and 1914, when The Drive, Pembroke Road and St Botolphs roads were laid out.

Industry and Agriculture

The industrial revolution largely passed Holmesdale by. Silk weaving was probably the most labour intensive industry there, taking advantage of natural springs at Greatness which rise in Millpond Wood (recently identified as an ancient peat bog) and which were already driving a corn mill. In 1764, this was inherited by Peter and Elizabeth Nouaille who were both descendants of Huguenot refugees, and who soon adapted the watermill to operate looms for weaving crepe silk. They built a terrace of ragstone cottages for some of their one hundred employees (tragically demolished in the 1960s), yet a Government report of 1816 records that their workforce also included children from the age of six working a 12-hour day. Their son Peter did not prosper to the same degree. The decline of the business was blamed on his personality, but it was the first importation of French silk in 1826 after a prohibition of nearly half a century which finally finished it off. A large portion of the mill was burned down in 1833; a section survives today though no longer operating as a mill.

Paper-making in Holmesdale was another small industry based on converted agricultural or fulling mills. The industry had moved up the Darent river valley since its founding at Darenth by John Spilman, the German papermaker, in 1588. By 1646 there was a paper mill at Eynsford, and by 1690 one at Shoreham. The paper was made from

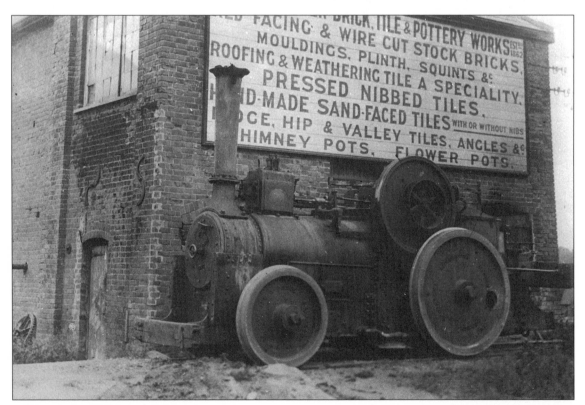

145 A steam engine provides power for the Dunton Green Brick, Tile and Pottery Works, later part of the Marley Tile estate (now a housing development).

146   Burrell's Forge in Underriver in the early part of this century.

rags of various qualities, and the cleanness of the Darent river water and its steady flow were essential for pulping and the final paper washing. The 1841 census records 12 paper makers and paper pickers in Shoreham, which had expanded to 70 employees working a 54-hour week in 1879.

Other industries were much smaller, probably only satisfying local demands. Brick and tile manufacture were primarily based in the Holmesdale valley. One early brickfield, however, was between Solefields Road and Weald Road, and despite, one imagines, its poor clay was able to take advantage of the demand from the growing town to the north. Chalk burning to produce lime for mortar and plaster took place at Polhill, and until the 1970s there was the skeleton of a whitening works on Chipstead Hill.

Leather was tanned in an outbuilding attached to Pickmoss, Otford, in the early 17th century, the tanhouse later moving to the site of The Grange, which replaced it in the early 19th century. Another tannery was on the London Road to the north of Riverhead. Improvements in road and then rail transportation soon made small industries such as this uncompetitive.

Large-scale intensive farming never reached Holmesdale, and the agricultural landscape of Holmesdale changed little over several centuries. When the artist Samuel Palmer was living at Water House in Shoreham between 1827 and 1835, the stories of his late night walks with friends to see the dawn at Underriver, or to buy a copy of a Gothic melodrama *The Mysteries of Udolpho* in Sevenoaks (setting out at 10 p.m.) belie some of our impressions of this period. His paintings show the valley with almost the same vibrant vitality as Van Gogh's Provence.

The year 1830 was a hard one for agricultural workers. The previous harvest had been bad, and the insensitivity of local landowners, some absentee, made conditions ripe for unrest. The disturbances of the mythical Captain Swing originated in East Kent, and the pattern of hayrick burning and threatening letters signed 'Swing' was repeated on a reduced scale at Holmesdale. Peter Nouaille, already unpopular for closing the silk mill, was among many farmers who received a Swing letter.

The Poor

The Swing riots may have had a part to play in the setting up of a Royal Commission in 1833 to look at the administration of the Poor Law. The commissioners found that farmers underpaid their workers, relying on the poor rates to make up the difference. John Brampton's correspondence with Lady Stanhope in 1770 indeed refers to a proposal to create workhouses in West Kent 60 years earlier, which local farmers feared would make hands short at harvest and hopping.

The Poor Law Amendment Act of 1834 resulted in 15 local parishes being grouped together in the Sevenoaks Union, and a workhouse was built halfway up St John's Hill. In the early years the new system was characterised by neglect and a degree of callousness; later the administration became more authoritarian, forbidding drink and tobacco, and even returning a gift of tea to a pauper from the rector's wife. The first building was demolished in 1846, although part of its surrounding wall remains on the south side of Camden Road, and the poor were moved to the new workhouse at Sundridge Chart (now a hospital). Westerham's poor joined them from their workhouse in Quebec Square.

$$\diamondsuit \text{ VII}$$

Postscript

Twentieth-Century Sevenoaks

The Decline and Fall of the Large House

Throughout Europe, the Great War of 1914-18 had devastated all classes of society. In the late 19th century, wealthy new arrivals to the town had built themselves large mansions, all of which relied on considerable numbers of servants. Wildernesse, at the time of Lord Hillingdon, employed almost 50 staff, mostly drawn from nearby Seal. The decimation of the Great War meant that many of these houses were no longer

viable, and thus when Lady Hillingdon died in 1921 Wildernesse became a country club with the present-day Wildernesse Golf Club in its grounds. Its magnificent stable building was saved from demolition in 1929 to become the Seal Laundry, while the house was bought in 1954 by the Royal London Society for the Blind as a school and was renamed Dorton House.

Large houses had always been suitable for conversion into schools. In 1906, Beechmont had become a boys' school when Multon Lambarde's

147   The Dunton Green Lido (seen *c*.1930) developed, like the Sevenoaks Open Air Swimming Bath at Greatness, from the centuries-old tradition of swimming in mill ponds. The enclosed Public Swimming Baths which opened in Eardley Road in 1914 does not seem to have diminished this Lido's use (at least in summer).

son forsook it for Bradbourne. After the war, Kippington House was a girls' school for 10 years until 1929, and Bulimba in Kippington was used as an infants' school in 1916 and then a girls' school. The most enduring conversions seem to have been further out from the town, as at Combe Bank, which became a girls' school in 1924, and at Ashgrove in 1932 (later West Heath). Other ventures were less immediately successful. Kippington House was an old people's home for a period after 1946 until the early 1980s when it was subdivided into flats and Brasted Place has had a similar conclusion after a period as a seminary. Kippington Grange has been an old people's home since 1952, while Craignure, or Kippington Court, built in 1900 and 'tudorised' externally in the 1920s, was given to Winston Churchill in 1946. He in turn gave it to the British Legion who renamed it Churchill Court, but it has since passed to a commercial body.

Greatness House did not even survive the First World War, being blown up as part of a wartime propaganda film. It had not been occupied by its owners, the Filmer family, for some time, and it is likely that the development of the north end of Sevenoaks and Bat and Ball (which had been part of its original estate) may have already spelled its end. The main millpond found another use as the Sevenoaks Open Air Swimming Pool from the end of the 19th century. This survived later competition from other open air baths in Brasted and Longford but its popularity declined after the Eardley Road swimming baths were opened in 1914.

Bulimba was demolished in 1928 having existed for barely a generation. Chipstead Place also had its central section demolished in the 1930s, and now the stable end survives at the east end and the ballroom at the west end, converted into two separate homes. Riverhill House, which is still owned by the Rogers family, may owe some of its vigour to the family allowing some of the less worthy Victorian additions to fall down.

Montreal was abandoned by the Amherst family in 1925, following the death of the 4th Earl. It was then bought by J.J. Runge of Kippington Court, who wanted to protect it from development, but his death in 1933 led to the demolition of the house and ensuing housing development on part of the estate. The obelisk commemorating the reunion of the three Amherst brothers in 1794 was absorbed into the garden of a house in Montreal Crescent, and a proposal to remove it to the United States in the 1960s was only just resisted.

Bradbourne was sold by Major William Gore Lambarde in 1927 and finally acquired by the New Ideal Homestead Company. The mid-18th-century lakes were given to the Urban District Council by an intermediate purchaser, Hugh Goff. The Hall survived for another 10 years, becoming more and more derelict, and my father has told me of illicit visits to play in its overgrown grounds when he was a young boy. It was finally demolished in 1937, and Nos.16-22 Robyns Way were built upon its site. Some of its ancillary buildings survive, as well as a few of the earlier eccentric owner Crawshay's druidical monoliths, the latter towering over the back gardens of several local houses.

Few great houses survived this period unchanged. Knole's survival was due to the foresight of the 4th Lord Sackville who gave the house together with an endowment to the National Trust in 1946, while retaining the right to occupy private sections of the building. St Clere and Chevening, the two double-pile houses, have also survived, St Clere still being lived in by Sir Mark Collet's descendants, the Norman family. Chevening House and its estate was left to the nation under a Trust set up in 1959 before the death of the 7th Earl Stanhope in 1966. The Prime Minister has to nominate who will live here, and for a while it was the private residence of the Prince of Wales, before being given for the use of the Foreign Secretary.

On a smaller scale, the architect Baillie Scott's original plans for houses in Kippington and Wildernesse between the wars show maids' bedrooms and sitting rooms and smaller secondary stairs in houses that were equivalent in size to some modern five-bedroom houses. These houses are not comparable with the architect's earlier work in Cambridge and elsewhere, and were carried out on a design-only commission for his builder son-in-law, Scott himself typically never visiting the site nor meeting the future occupants.

The World Wars

The two world wars involved the whole district in the way that no other war had done since the Civil War. Although no bombing came nearer than Knockholt in the First World War, the threat was always there. The great loss of manpower both during the war, and immediately afterwards, caused many adjustments, particularly in the supply of domestic staff.

By the Second World War, there were more physical preparations for the war. My grandfather was one of the first in Sevenoaks to build an air raid shelter in his garden in Kippington Road in the late 1930s. Aerial bombardment was followed by V1 doodlebugs and V2 rocket attacks. The V1s destroyed Beechmont as well as the Iron Church in South Park that had been used while Kippington Church was being built. Another poignant reminder is the grave memorial in Riverhead churchyard to a family with two young children killed by a V1.

The Motor Car

The motor car had made its first appearance in Sevenoaks by the end of the 19th century, although no-one could guess the effect it would have on those empty streets we see in Victorian photographs. At the close of the century many new buildings, including the Council Offices, were being built with stables, which within a decade or two would become garages. Traffic in the town and along the valley floor would one day become desparately congested, prompting by-passes and motorways. Car parks, windswept areas of asphalt, would cover the fields of *Bligh's*, the gardens of the *Crown Hotel* and the stables and redundant brewery buildings of Suffolk Place. Meanwhile, the effect of this new competition on the railways would lead to the loss of the Westerham Branch Line in the 1960s. Sevenoaks has survived far better than most towns in this process thanks to its precarious position on a ridge, protected by Knole Park to the east and the

148   The Iron, or Tin, Church at the junction of South Park with Granville Road, photographed around 1920. This had been built by W.S. Thompson prior to the completion of St Mary's Kippington, and was destroyed by a V1 doodlebug in the Second World War.

149 Golding's Brewery in Cramptons Road, Bat and Ball was a formidable structure, which, together with the Suffolk Place Brewery in the Lower High Street and the Black Eagle Brewery in Westerham, went a long way towards slaking local thirsts.

150 Otford High Street in the 19th century, showing the Parish Workhouse of 1790 on the extreme right, which by 1835 had been converted into three houses. Beyond is a triple-dormered 17th-century oak-framed building, one part of which was occupied by the village blacksmith who had his forge in the adjoining barn.

railway to the west. A deadly scheme for an Eastern Way, which would break forever that prospect of parkland and calm within a minute or two's walk from the town centre, has been shelved temporarily. Meanwhile other schemes are being put forward to lessen the use of the private car through reducing public car parks, increasing town centre bus services, and promoting dedicated cycle paths.

Town and Village Growth

Sevenoaks has continued to grow, primarily in developments of small suburban roads. The middle-class villa was the pattern for the late Victorian and Edwardian houses of The Drive and the ragstone Holmesdale and Serpentine Roads, for example, which were based on Tub's Hill railway station, while the artisan terraced housing

of Moor Road was being built near Bat and Ball. The latter was primarily for rent, although more imaginative co-operative housing was built at St Botolph's Avenue in 1906 designed by Raymond Unwin (the Garden City pioneer) and at Frank Swanzy's 1905 Holyoak Terrace, off Oakhill Road.

Many of the new roads also sold individual plots, and the old roads sold infill plots, to allow purchasers to build their own houses, such as along Kippington and Oakhill Roads primarily between the wars. Often these plots would come with covenants defining the minimum value of the house to be built and the setback from the highway, giving the new roads a recognisable character. The White Hart estates, formerly Knole land, at the south end of Sevenoaks, called for frontage hedges or low walls. These houses date mainly from the 1930s and 1940s, while many later developments, such as Beaconsfield, off Brittains Lane, and Chesterfield Drive in Riverhead, require the more sterile open lawn effect that gives no transition between public and private spaces.

Public housing began to be built during the First World War by the Urban District Council, when it bought land belonging to the former Greatness House. These first council houses are quite impressive, a record not matched in the 1920s and 1930s estates on land bought from the Wildernesse estate in the Hillingdon area. New developments continued after the Second World War on former Bradbourne and Kippington estate lands, and on the lands of several properties in the Solefields area. These days, new housing is provided through Housing Associations in smaller and more piecemeal developments, which have included blocks of flats and sheltered housing, forms which are often out of sympathy with the townscape.

The villages have suffered much worse from suburban growth, retaining their original small centres while growing 10 or 20 fold in area. Otford and Kemsing grew towards and finally joined one another along the Pilgrims' Way, Seal

151 H.G. Wells's Cycle and Motorcycle Shop in Otford, around 1924. The father of the owner had founded the St Johns Cycle Depot at the turn of the century, and had named his son after the founder of science fiction (who coincidentally had briefly lived in Eardley Road in Sevenoaks).

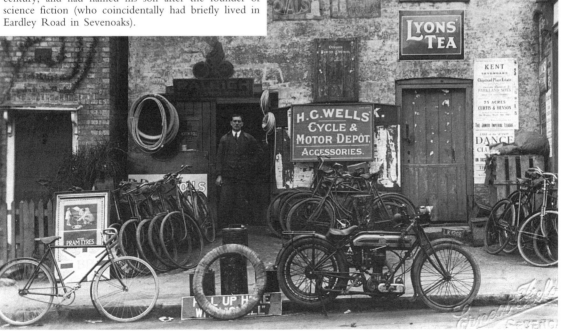

152   Dunton Green bus station.

was almost joined onto Bat and Ball, while Riverhead was in danger of being absorbed in all directions. The creation of the Green Belt after the Second World War halted this ribbon development, and froze the new outer limits.

Most pre-Green Belt rural development was like this, but Knatts Valley, north of Kemsing, is rather unusual. Plots of land on the floor of a dry river valley were built on between the wars with owner-built shacks, some of which still survive and have interesting features. Meanwhile Broadhoath, near Bitchet Green, is an estate of houses, arranged in a circle around a shared green, in an idealised vision of a community.

Local Government

Local government was only six years old at the start of this century, and has since grown to wield tremendous influence. Where the Vestry was exclusive and perhaps patronising, local government, for all its faults, works along democratic lines. District and county councils have been responsible for the town centre's new public buildings, the new library and swimming baths, and the rebuilt District Council offices. Through local plans and the exercise of planning controls they have had a hand in new commercial and

other buildings, although this was not enough to stop the building of the town's first and last 'skyscraper' at Tub's Hill in the 1960s. The removal of the market from the town centre, after the Urban District Council had acquired the rights in 1925, continued the zeal for neatness that the Victorians had begun.

The District Council, through compulsory purchase, is now the major landowner and the driving force behind the new town centre development proposed for Bligh's Meadow. The proposals are now not as large-scale as they have been at various stages of the last thirty or so years, but they lack the imagination and humanity that the 19th-century benefactors might have given to the proposals, as the council sees its role more as developer rather than visionary. In the process, Brewery Lane's fine yellow and red brick Victorian workshop has gone, as well as other buildings at the rear of the Daws site and the less obviously missable 1930s Bus Station, together with the chance to create a true town square.

Conservation

The awareness of our built and rural heritage has grown tremendously this century, paradoxically at the same time that so much has been lost.

Octavia Hill, the founder of the National Trust, was from Crockham Hill and was responsible for the purchase of lands at Toys Hill and Ide Hill in 1899. The National Trust now also owns Knole, Quebec House and Chartwell, as well as much of Chiddingstone village and Oldbury Hill.

William Morris's work in protecting churches from over-zealous repair and reinterpretative re-building has taken a long time to spread to other buildings, although the system of making statu-tory lists of important historic buildings now warns interested bodies of changes to the most historic buildings. One problem is that many medieval timber frames are concealed behind much later facades, as Anthony Stoyel and his researchers found in Otford and other parts of Holmesdale. Statutory protection came too late to save the Greatness Mill cottages, and even these days some buildings of quality in the area are not protected and are at risk.

The first half of this century was the most dangerous for the town, when large sections of the town and in particular the north end of the High Street were demolished and rebuilt. Between Bank Street and Pembroke Road there are today only two older buildings left, *Bligh's Hotel* and No.107 High Street. One very large section, from 121 to 133 High Street, seems the work of one 1930s developer, with the recurring theme of Tudor-style gabled projections. No.125 (the estate agents, Ibbetts), is the best of these with a very courteous design feature in its splayed corner, corbelled above, allowing one to turn the corner more easily. This was perhaps suggested by the splayed corner of the recently demolished fine Victorian workshop in Brewery Lane. It was also during this period that the Victorian Market House was, in 1924, converted into public lava-tories, an ignominy from which it was rescued in the 1970s.

There were plans by the County Council in the 1950s to widen the High Street opposite the Market House to align the north and south ends of the road. This would have made both ends of the High Street less intimate and more amor-phous, and the Sevenoaks Preservation Society (now the Sevenoaks Society) was reformed in 1952 to resist this.

Outside the town centre there were tremen-dous dangers, too. A new town of 20,000 people in Whitley forest had been a serious possibility in 1939, when it was defeated by local outcry and perhaps also the start of the war. The post-war Green Belt came in time to save the north side of Bradbourne Vale Road, the west of Brittains Lane, the remaining half of the Montreal estate, and Blackhall Farm from development.

Bibliography

Anckorn, Gordon, *A Sevenoaks Camera* (1979)

Anckorn, Gordon, *Sevenoaks Memories* (1984)

Baker, F.A., *The Story of Sundridge Old Hall*

Barton, G. and Tong M., *Underriver: Samuel Palmer's Golden Valley* (1995)

Bolton, Arthur T., *The Architecture of Robert and James Adam* (1922)

Bowden, V.E., *The Story of Kemsing in Kent*

Box, E.G., 'Notes on Some West Kent Roads in Early Maps and Road Books', *Archaeologia Cantiana*, vol.43

Box, E.G., 'Notes on the History of Saxon Otford', *Archaeologia Cantiana*, vol.43

Chalklin, C.W., *Seventeenth Century Kent: A Social and Economic History* (1965)

Clarke, P. and Stoyel, A., *Otford in Kent: A History* (1975)

Clarke, R.D., *The Medieval History of St John the Baptist, Sevenoaks* (1971)

Donald, Archie, *The Posts of Sevenoaks 1085-1985* (1992)

DuBoulay, F.R.H., 'Late-continued demesne farming at Otford', *Archaeologia Cantiana*, vol.73 (1959)

DuBoulay, F.R.H., 'The Assembly of an Estate: Knole in Sevenoaks, c.1275-1528', *Archaeologia Cantiana*, vol.89 (1974)

Dunlop, J., *The Pleasant Town of Sevenoaks: A History* (1964)

Edwards, Jane, *Her Recollections of Old Sevenoaks* (1985)

Everitt, A.M., *Landscape & Community in England* (1985)

Everitt, A.M., *Continuity & Colonization: The Evolution of Kentish Settlement* (1986)

Glover, J., *The Place Names of Kent* (1976)

Gravett, K., *Timber and Brick Building in Kent* (1971)

Haigh, Diane, *Baillie Scott: The Artistic House* (1996)

Harris, J., *History of Kent; an exact topography and description of the county* (1719)

Hasted, Edward, *The history and topographical survey of the county of Kent* (1797-1801)

H.M.S.O., *Geological Survey of Great Britain: Geology of the Country around Sevenoaks* (1969)

Hussey, Christopher, 'St Clere, Kent', *Country Life* (March 1962)

Ide Hill Society, *A Village in Kent, Ide Hill Past and Present* (1983)

Jackson, T.G., *Recollections of Thomas Graham Jackson* (1950)

Jackson-Stops, Gervase, *Knole* (1986)

Jessup, Frank W., *A History of Kent* (1995)

Knocker, H.W., 'The valley of Holmesdale: its evolution and development', *Archaeologia Cantiana*, vol.31 (1915)

Knocker, H.W., 'Sevenoaks Manor, Church and Market', *Archaeologia Cantiana*, vol.38 (1926)

Lambarde, W., *A perambulation of Kent: containing the description, historie and customes of that shire* (1576, repr. 1970)

Margary, I.D., *Roman Ways in the Weald* (1965)

Mason, R.T., *Framed Buildings of the Weald* (1969)

Meates, G.W., *Lullingstone Roman Villa* (1955)

Mills, Marian, *Your Most Dutyful Servant: Eighteenth Century Chevening Recreated* (1992)

Mills, Marian, *A Riverhead Century 1894-1994* (1994)

Morris, J. (ed.), *Domesday Book: Kent* (1983)

Morris, R., *Churches in the Landscape* (1989)

Newman, John, *Buildings of England: West Kent and the Weald* (1991)

Newton, Jill, *Chiddingstone: An Historical Exploration* (1985)

Pearson, Sarah, *The Medieval Houses of Kent: An Historical Analysis* (1994)

Pearson, S., Barnwell, P.S. and Adams, A., *A Gazetteer of Medieval Houses in Kent* (1994)

Philp, B.J., *Excavations in the Darenth Valley, Kent* (1984)

Pike, E., Curryer, C. and Moore, U.K., *The Story of Walthamstow Hall* (1973)

Platt, Colin, *The Great Rebuildings of Tudor and Stuart England* (1994)

Pyke, J.A., 'Danes Trench and prehistoric land division in the Upper Darent valley', *Archaeologia Cantiana*, vol.94 (1978)

Quiney, A., *Kent Houses* (1991)

Raybould, G., *A Short History of Bessels Green* (1981)

Raybould, G., *Combe Bank: A History* (1986)

Richards, Frank, *Old Sevenoaks* (1901)

Sackville-West, Vita, *Knole and the Sackvilles* (repr. 1991)

Saynor, J. and White, M., *Shoreham: A Village in Kent* (1990)

Scragg, Brian, *Sevenoaks School: A History* (1993)

Sevenoaks Society, *100 Years' Growth in Sevenoaks Services* (1994)

Smithers, D.W., *A History of Knockholt in the County of Kent* (1991)

Standen, H.W., *Kippington in Kent* (1958)

Stoyel, A., *Otford's Medieval Court Hall*

Stoyel, A., *Numbers 99 and 101 High Street and the former Market Place* (1982)

Thompson, Edwin, *Sevenoaks Recollections* (1994)

Ward, Gordon, *Sevenoaks Essays* (1980)

Webber, M., 'St Nicholas's Church, Sevenoaks', *Oxford Archaeological Unit Annual Report* (1994)

Witney, K.P., *The Jutish Forest: A study of the Weald of Kent from A.D.450-1380* (1976)

Witney, K.P., *The Kingdom of Kent* (1982)

White, J.T., *The Parklands of Kent* (1975)

Index

———◆◆◆◆———

Bold references refer to illustrations

Adam of Usk, 32
agriculture, 4,6
almshouses, *see* hospitals
Amherst Arms, 43
Amherst family, 63, 70, 89, 90, 94, 101, 111, 118
Andredswald, 5, 26
Ashgrove House, 74, 96, **97**, 118
Austen family, 64, 66, 76, 98, 103

Baillie Scott, M.H., 118
Bank Street, Sevenoaks, 123
Baptist Church, Sevenoaks, 80-3
Bat and Ball station, 101, 103, 113
Battle of Otford (775), 24; (1016), 26
Beaconsfield, Sevenoaks, 121
Becket, Archbishop Thomas, 22, 32
Becket's Well, Otford, 22, **32**
Beechmont House, 96, **97**, 118, 119
Bessels Green, 16, 54, 55, 66, 69; Baptist Chapel, 55
Bethlehem Hospital, 85
Bitchet Green, 16, 122
Black Boy Inn, **88**, 89, 108
Black Death, 39-40
Black Eagle Brewery, Westerham, 38
Blackhall, 3, 16, 35, 42, 90, 123
Bligh's Hotel, **34**, 80, **83**, **84**, **86**, 119, 122, 123
Boleyn family, 41, 49
Bore Place, 16
Bosville family, 48, 50, 66, 108
boundaries, 6, 13, 24, 31
Bourchier, Archbishop Thomas, 45, 78
Box House, Kemsing 21
Bradbourne, 21, 40, 42, 48, 50, 55, **64**, 90, 96, 103, 113, 118
Brasted, **12**, 13, 16, 18, 28, 33, **38**, 47, 67, 68; church, **12**, 20, 21; Place, **64**, 70, 74, 99; station, **103**
Brasted Chart, 17
Brewery Lane, Sevenoaks, 122, 123
brickmaking, **5**, 10, **114**

Brittains Lane, 121
Brittains Manor, 35, 40, 42, 63
Brook Place, Riverhead, 21, 47, 63; *see also* Montreal
Bubblestone Road, Otford, 47
Bulimba, Kippington Road, **100**, 101, 118
burials, 8, 9, 10, 13, 38

Cade, Jack, **18**, 40-41
Carrick Grange, **100**
Castle Farm, Shoreham, 4
chantry, Sevenoaks, 38, 39, 47, 78
Chapel Wood, Seal, 21
Charn, The, Otford, 7, 13
chartland, 1, 17
Chartwell, 123
Chequers Inn, Sevenoaks, **34**, 36
Chesterfield Drive, Riverhead, 121
Chevening, 1, 13, **14**, 21, **59**; Church, 20, 21, 28, 47; House, 50-1, 57, 60, **61**, 118
Chiddingstone, 16, 28, **42**, 123; Castle, 41; Church, 20, 21, 57
Chipstead, 13, 16, 24, **25**, **68**; Place, 3, **60**, **71**, **72**, 73, 118
Church Field, Riverhill, 22
churches, 30-2, 38, 39, 47, 110-12; *see also* individual churches
Churchill Court, *see* Kippington Court
Civil War, 52
Clare family, 28, **38**
Codsheath, 23, 24
Coldharbour, Bessels Green, 16; Penshurst, 16
Colgate, John, 55
Combe Bank, **61**, 62, 70, 118
Congregational Church, St John's Hill, 90, **111**; church hall, Hollybush Lane, **112**
Copstone, Otford, 4, 16
Cory Yokes, Knockholt, 21
Cottage Hospital, Sevenoaks, 103, **108**
courts, 24, 29, 30
Cranmer, Archbishop Thomas, 47

Cray, River, 11
Crockham Hill, 2, 123
Crown Hotel, Sevenoaks, 79, **80**
Crown Inn, Chipstead, **25**

Danes Trench, Polhill, 5, 26
Darent, river, 1, 3, 11, 14
Darenth Roman Villa, 7
Devey, George, 17
Dibden, 17, 21, 55
Domesday Book, 27, 28
Donnington Manor, Dunton Green, 4
Dorset Arms, Sevenoaks, 41, 80
Dorset Street, Sevenoaks, 36, 37
Downs, North, 1
Drive, The, Sevenoaks, 120
Dunton Green, 16, 54, 103, **117**

Edenbridge, 10, 18, 21
Edmund Ironside, 26
Edwards, Jane, 37, 75
Eleanor, Princess, 37, 38
Elizabeth I, 47, 48
Emily Jackson Hip Hospital, **104**
Eynsford, 11, 17, **20**, 28, 69; castle, 32; church, 20,
     21, 31

Fairfield Close, Kemsing, 38
fairs, 38
Farnaby family, 51, 52, 63, 64, 66
Farningham, 14, 41; church, 20, 21; Iron-Age farm,
     6; Roman Villa, 9
Fawke Common, 2
feudal system, 26, 28
Fiennes, James, 40-41
Filston, Shoreham, 14, **20**, 28, 41, 47
flint, 1, **2**, 7
fords, 17, **20**
Frankfield, Seal Chart, 52
Frith, John, 47-48
Frog Farm, Otford, 7

Gallows Common, 48, 114
Gault Clay, 1, **5**
gavelkind, 28, 29
Goathurst Common, 2
Godden Green, 53, 54
granaries, 10
Great Cockerhurst, Shoreham, 16
Greatness, 26, 40, 55, **62**, 63, **72**, 118, 121; Chapel,
     see St John the Baptist Hospital
Greenhill, Otford, 3, 4, 7
Greensand, lower, 1, 2

hall houses, 29, 30, **35**, 44
Halstead, **2**, 11, 16, 28; church, 20, 21
Harold, King, 27

Hasted, 69, **70**, 74
Hearth Tax, 56
Henden, Ide Hill, 30, 41
Henry VIII, 45, 47
Hever, 18, 28, 47; castle, 41; church, 21
High Street, Sevenoaks, no.101, **36**, **37**
hillforts, 4, 5, **8**
Hillingdon, 121
hollow road, Oldbury, **8**
hollow way, Childsbridge Lane, 5
Holmesdale Road, Sevenoaks, 120
Holy Field, Riverhill, 22
Holyoak Terrace, Sevenoaks, 120
Holywell Shaw, Westerham, 22
Hosey Common, 2
hospitals, 20, 21, 22, 33, 34, 47, 63, 103, **104**, **108**
Hubbards Hill, 2
Hullberry, Lullingstone, 5, 14
Hundred of Codsheath, 23, 24
hundredal courts, *see* courts

Ice Age, 1, 3
Ide Hill, 54; school, 109
Ightham, 68; church, 20; Mote, 41, 57
iron, 4, 5, 6
Iron Church, South Park, **119**
Ivy Hatch, 16, 54

Jackson: Emily, 104; Thomas, 104, **105**, 109, 112
jail, 30, 37, 48, 49

Kemsing, 13, 14, 16, 26, 27, 28, 33, **54**, 121, 122;
     castle, **21**, 32; church, 20, 21, 23, 31, 33, 38, 47;
     Roman Villa, 7; school, 109
Kippington, St Mary's Church, 103
Kippington Court, 74, 101, 118
Kippington Grange, 101, 118
Kippington House, 14, 35, 42, 52, 55, **63**, 118;
     Lodge, 73, **74**
Knatts Valley, 1, 122
Knockholt, 11, 16; church, **16**; House, **99**
Knole House, 16, 21, 35, 37, 40, 42, **45**-7, **49**, 50,
     52, 56, 57, 59, **71**, 89, 94, **95**, **96**, 118, 123;
     Park, **6**, 40, 119

Lady Boswell's School, **82**, 108
Lamb Inn, Sundridge, **30**
Lambarde family, 47, 53, 66, 76, 80, 96, 104, 111,
     117, 118
Lathe of Sutton-at-Hone, 23
Leigh, 17
lime burning, **4**
Lock's Yard, Sevenoaks, 36
Locks Bottom Road, *see* Seal Hollow Road
Longford, Dunton Green, 17, 27, **67**, 69
Lullingstone, 7, 16, 18, 28; castle, 42, 46; park, 4, 6,
     40; Roman Villa, 7, **9**, 10, 11; St Botolph's

Church, 20, 21; St John the Baptist Church, 10, 20, 21
Lyndhurst Drive, Sevenoaks, 3

manorial courts, *see* courts
Maplescombe Church, 1, 20, 39
market cross, 21, 35, 36
Market House, Sevenoaks, **88**, 123
markets: Brasted, 36, **38**; boundary, 24; Chipstead, 24; Kemsing, 37; Otford, 24; Sevenoaks, 21, 24, **33**, **34**, 35-7; Westerham, 24, 36, 38
Maywood, Bradbourne Road, Sevenoaks, 101, 103
Medway river, 5, 6
Millpond Wood, Greatness, 3, 4
mills, 28-30; Bradbourne, 29; Brasted, 28; Chipstead, 29; Eynsford, **20**, 28; Greatness, 28, 29, 30, 123; Longford, 28, 29; Otford, 28, **29**; Shoreham, 28, **29**, 48; Sundridge, 28, **30**; Whitley, 28, 29
Milton, Shoreham, 21
Milton, Seal, 28
minster churches, 19, 21
moated sites, **18**, 41
Montreal Crescent, 118
Montreal House, **62**, 74, 118, 123; Park, 18
Moor Road, Sevenoaks, 120
Morants Court, 30, 40

Nizels, 16
Noah's Ark, Kemsing, 18
Norman Street, 54
Nouaille family, 55, 63, 114, 116

Oakhill Road, Sevenoaks, 120
Oak Lane, Sevenoaks, 35
Oaks Cross, Underriver, 21
Odo, Bishop of Bayeux, 28
Offa, King of Mercia, 24
Old Post Office, Upper High Street, Sevenoaks, 58, 76, **77**
Oldbury Hill, 2, 3, 5, 6, **8**, 14, 28, 33, 68, 123
One Tree Hill, 10
Otford, 7, 11, 13, 17, 18, 19, 24, 26, **27**, 28, 35, 39, 48, 59, 73, 106, **120**, 121, 123; church, 4, 7, 13, 20, 21, **31**, 33, 47, 69; Court Hall, 29-30, **31**; Manor House, 30, 33, 40; Mount, 4, 5; Palace, 42, **46**; pond, **12**, **27**; Roman villas, 7; school, 109
Otford Weald, 18
Outrams, London Road, Sevenoaks, 47

Packhorse Road, Bessels Green, 3
pagan practices, 9, 10, 13, 22, 23
Palmer, Samuel, 115
Panthurst, Sevenoaks Weald, 2, 47
paper mills, 114-15
parishes, 6
Park Grange, Sevenoaks, **33**, 35, 53

Park Lane, Seal, 69
Park Place, **52**, 53, 58, 70, 74
parks, 40, 47
Peasants Revolt, 40
Pembroke Road, Sevenoaks, 123
Pemley Court, *see* Bradbourne
Penfield, Seal, 38
Penshurst, 16, **17**, 18, 28, 29, 30, 37; church, 20, 21, 30; Place, 41, 47; Rectory, 57
pest houses, 108
Pilgrims Way, 3, 13, 33, 121
Plaxtol, 16
Plegstow, Twitton, 16
Polhill, **4**, 5, 13
Polhill family, 48, 52, 56, 59, 68, 70
poor houses, 48
Preston, Shoreham, 14, 19, 21

Quebec House, Westerham, 123

ragstone, Kentish, 2
railway, 1, 101-3
Red House, High Street, Sevenoaks, 64, **65**
Redman's Place, Sevenoaks, **91**
Riverhead, 17, **19**, 24, **43**, 56, **57**, 68, 121, 122; church, **19**, **111**, 119
Riverhill, 16, 69
Riverhill House, 2, 59-**60**, 68, 98, 118
roadstone, 2
Rogers family, 98, 118
Roman villas, 6, 7, 13
Romshed, Underriver, 2, 16, 22, 34, 40, 41, 53
Royal Oak, Sevenoaks, 76, 80
Rumstead, *see* Romshed
Rye, Dunton Green, 18
Rye fish route, 24

Sackville: Edward, 52; Richard, 49; Thomas, 49; family, 58, 63, 67, 76, 78, 94, 96, 118
Sackville-West, Vita, 42
St Botolph's Avenue, Sevenoaks, 120
St Clere, Kemsing, 21, **51**, 57, 98, 103, 118
St Edith, 21
St Edith's Well, Kemsing, *see* wells
St John the Baptist Hospital, Greatness, 20, 21, 22, 33, 47, 63
St John's Hill, 3
St Julian, 22, 96
St Julian's, 2, 22
St Mary's Church, Kippington, *see* Kippington
St Nicholas' Church, Sevenoaks, 20, 21, **22**, 31, 38, 39, 48, 79, 110, 111
sarsen stones, 4, 31
schools, 108-10; *see also* individual schools
Seal, **15**, 16, 26, 27, 28, 33, 38, 68, 109, 117, 119; church, 20, 21, 110
Seal Chart, 17, 47; church, 111

Seal Hollow Road, Sevenoaks, 1, **6**, 68, 69, 70, 90

Sepham, Shoreham, 14, 24, 28, 29

Serpentine Road, Sevenoaks, 120

Sevenoaks Chronicle, **106**

Sevenoaks Common, 2

Sevenoaks Manor, 29

Sevenoaks Park House, *see* Park Place

Sevenoaks School, 34, 35, 66, 108, 109

Sevenoaks Weald, 18, 54; church, 111

seven oak trees, 16, **25**

Sevenoke, William, 34, 35, 48, 66

Shambles, **35**, **36**, 37, **81**

Shenden, Sevenoaks, 17, **18**

Shipbourne Church, 20

Shoreham, 13, 14, **15**, 19, 26, 29, 55, 69, 70, 106; castle, 32; church, 13, 19, 20, 21, 31, 39, 69; Holly Place, 43, 58; Roman villa, 7; school, 109

Shoreham, William de, 32

silk weaving, 114

Six Bells Lane, Sevenoaks, 56, **78**, 103

Solefields, 17, **18**

Solefields Road, Sevenoaks, 121

Somerden, Chiddingstone, 16

Springhead, Kemsing, 7

springs, 9, 13, 34

Squerryes, Westerham, 5, 29

Stanhope family, 60-2, 67, 70, 116, 118

Stiddolphs, *see* Wildernesse

Stone Cross, Seal, 21

Stonepitts, Seal Chart, 2

Stone Street, Seal, 16, 68; St Lawrence Church, 111

Stonewall, Chiddingstone, 3

Streatfeild family, 70

Styant's Bottom, Seal Chart, 33

Sundridge, 13, 16, 28, 34, 54, 55, 67, 68; church, 2, 20, 21; Fever Hospital, 108; Old Hall, 43, **44**; Well Cottage, 43

tanneries, 10

Tanners Cross, Seal, 21

Textus Roffensis, 20, 31

Theobald, Thomas, 32

Timberden, Shoreham, 29

timber frame, 42

tithings, 24

Titsey, 10

Tonbridge, 28

Toys Hill, 2, 3, 54

trackways, prehistoric, 3, 6

transhumance, 6

Tub's Hill Station, 102, 114, 120

Turner's Nurseries, Tonbridge Road, Sevenoaks, **18**

turnpike roads, 67-70, 106

Twitton, 16

Underriver, 16, **115**; House, 56, 99

Upsepham, *see* Sepham

utilities, 106-7

Vikings, 23, 26

Vine, The, **25**, 66, 68, **93**; Baptist Church, **41**, 66

Vine Court, **113**

Vine Lodge, **101**

Wallington, Surrey, 13, 23

Walthamshow Hall School, 109-10

Warham, Archbishop of Canterbury, 46, 47

water supply, 2

Weald, 5

Weardale Manor, Toys Hill, 96

Webbs Alley, Sevenoaks, 36, 46

well chapels, 21, 22; Becket's Well, Otford, 22, **32**; Greatness, 34; St Edith's Well, Kemsing, 22, **23**, 33

wells, 21, 22

Wesley, John, 79

West End Dairy, Sevenoaks, **79**

Westerham, 11, 18, 23, 24, 28, 29, 38, **39**, 41, 56, 67, 68, 116; church, 20, 21, **39**; Green, 55; Pitts Cottage, 58; school, 109

Westerham Hill, 1

Westerham Road, Bessels Green, Chevening, 3

West Heath School, *see* Ashgrove House

White Hart Inn, Sevenoaks, **25**

White House, High Street, Sevenoaks, 75, **78**, **90**

Wickham, Otford, 16

Wickham Field, Otford, 7

Wickhurst, 40

Wildernesse House, **73**, **98**, 117

William I, 27, 28

windmills: Knotts Smock Mill, **83**, Sevenoaks Common, 85, Sevenoaks Weald, 85

Wolfe, General James, 63

Woodlands Church, 1, 20, 21, 39, 40

Wrotham, 28

Wyatt's Rebellion, 48

Yaldham, 14

yokes, 29

Ordnance Survey map of Sevenoaks, 1870